HISTORIC PHOTOS OF
UNIVERSITY OF
GEORGIA FOOTBALL

TEXT AND CAPTIONS BY PATRICK GARBIN

TURNER
PUBLISHING COMPANY

HISTORIC PHOTOS OF
UNIVERSITY OF
GEORGIA FOOTBALL

Turner Publishing Company
200 4th Avenue North • Suite 950
Nashville, Tennessee 37219
(615) 255-2665

www.turnerpublishing.com

Historic Photos of University of Georgia Football

Copyright © 2010 Turner Publishing Company

Library of Congress Control Number: 2010926732

ISBN: 978-1-59652-577-1

Printed in China

10 11 12 13 14 15 16 17—0 9 8 7 6 5 4 3 2 1

CONTENTS

ACKNOWLEDGMENTS...VII

PREFACE VIII

LAYING THE FOUNDATION TOWARD PROMINENCE
    (1892–1938) 1

ERA OF THE INNOVATIVE "LITTLE ROUND MAN"
    (1939–1960) 39

VINCE WHO?
    (1961–1970) 105

THE BUMPY ROAD TO PERFECTION
    (1971–1980)..141

NOTES ON THE PHOTOGRAPHS 201

Coach Vince Dooley concludes his first regular season at Georgia by receiving a victory ride following a 7–0 win over Georgia Tech. He is met by Coach Bobby Dodd at midfield of Sanford Stadium. Dodd and his Yellow Jackets won 11 of 15 games against the Bulldogs from 1949 to 1963 before losing three times straight (1964-66) to the coaching legend Dooley.

ACKNOWLEDGMENTS

This volume, *Historic Photos of University of Georgia Football,* is the result of the cooperation and efforts of many individuals and organizations. It is with great thanks that we acknowledge the valuable contribution of the University of Georgia at Athens for their generous support.

PREFACE

Less than six years after its inception, football at the University of Georgia was almost abolished in 1897, following the untimely and tragic death of a player. Anti-football legislation, which would have outlawed college football in the state, nearly became law.

More than 110 years later, following countless Georgia football victories, many finishes being ranked in the final polls, numerous All-Americans, 14 conference titles, 5 national championships according to at least one recognized poll, and 2 Heisman Trophy winners, it is difficult for me and thousands of other fans to comprehend what life would be like without Georgia Bulldogs football. Following the anti-football scare, the sport persisted at the school through both the best and worst of times, climaxing in 1980 with an undefeated, untied, and undisputed national title—the first of its kind at the University of Georgia in any sport.

The photographs on the following pages, primarily consisting of Georgia players, reflect the rich history of the football program from its uncertain beginning through its most successful season. With the exception of touching up imperfections that have accrued with the passage of time and cropping where necessary, no changes have been made. The focus and clarity of many images are limited by the technology and the ability of the photographer at the time they were taken.

The historic images are divided into four different eras. The first section looks at the team from its beginnings in the 1890s through 1938. During this period of 45 seasons, most of which were winning campaigns, Georgia had a startling 19 head coaches, none of whom lasted more than 10 years. The second section is an era under the leadership of only one head coach—the legendary Wally Butts. Coach Butts guided the Bulldogs from 1939 to 1960. Each of the final two sections covers a period of 10 seasons. The third focuses on the unremarkable, three-year reign of Coach Johnny Griffith and the first several years of a young and little-known Coach Vince Dooley. The final section takes a look at the turbulent 1970s, ending with the team's ultimate accomplishment in college football—finishing the season ranked number-one in the entire country.

Like many of you, I have seen hundreds of Georgia football photos over the years, scattered in various books, magazines, newspapers, and elsewhere, some of which are included here. But never before has there been a book quite like this one—with so many images so well organized, many of which have seldom been seen by the general public, and devoted solely to University of Georgia football.

Whether you are a college football fan, history buff, or member of the Bulldog Nation, I hope you enjoy this century-long look back at a unique university football program. These photographs remind us that what was nearly outlawed became one of the most acclaimed and tradition-filled college football teams of all time.

—*Patrick Garbin*

Georgia's "Dream Backfield" of 1942: (From left to right) halfback-fullback Frank Sinkwich, halfback Charley Trippi, fullback Dick McPhee, and halfback Lamar "Racehorse" Davis. Sinkwich won the Heisman that season, Trippi would finish runner-up four years later, Davis was a record-breaking receiver and returner, and McPhee opened holes for all of them to run through.

LAYING THE FOUNDATION TOWARD PROMINENCE

(1892–1938)

The beginnings of football at the University of Georgia can be traced to the fall of 1891 when Dr. Charles Herty decided to bring the sport to his alma mater after observing a game in Baltimore. Herty soon organized a team, but no opposition in the area existed. Finally, Mercer College of Macon, Georgia, took interest in the sport and fielded a squad.

On January 30, 1892, the visiting team was no match for the mighty Red and Black as Georgia prevailed in its first game 50–0 on the school's Alumni Athletic Field, later renamed Herty Field. Evidently, the final score should have been 60–0, but the official scorer made two trips to Athens' Broad Street Dispensary during the game for "refreshments" and missed two touchdowns, counting four points each, and a successful conversion, counting for two.

The first two decades of Georgia football were quite irregular. A Southern Intercollegiate Athletic Association (S.I.A.A.) championship was won in 1896, but then the death of Richard Vonalbade Gammon, a fullback for the Red and Black, ensued the very next season, which nearly led to outlawing the sport. This was followed by mostly losing campaigns during the early part of the 1900s.

In 1910, Coach Alex Cunningham and halfback Bob McWhorter left the Gordon Institute of Barnesville, Georgia, came to Athens, and instantly revolutionized football at the University of Georgia into one of the better programs in the South. His 10-year coaching stint interrupted by World War I in 1917 and 1918, Cunningham had just one losing season in eight campaigns. McWhorter is still considered by some as the school's most valuable football player of all time.

The Roaring Twenties were certainly that for the program. In 1920, Georgia captured its second S.I.A.A. championship (and adopted the nickname "Bulldogs") and claimed a national title in 1927. From 1928 to 1937, Coach Harry Mehre had an admirable tenure, but it was not quite good enough for some of the influential alumni and the coach resigned. Joel Hunt followed Mehre, but he was removed after only a single season.

As the 1930s neared to a close, Georgia football desperately wanted to return to its heyday. Although the upcoming 1939 season would mark the Bulldogs' third head coach in as many years, UGA officials were confident they would finally find the right man for the job.

Pictured is the first University of Georgia football team. In 1892, the Red and Black defeated Mercer 50–0 in Athens and then lost to Auburn 10–0 in Atlanta. Frank "Si" Herty (first row, second from left), cousin of UGA football's founder and first coach Dr. Charles Herty, scored the first points for Georgia on a touchdown run.

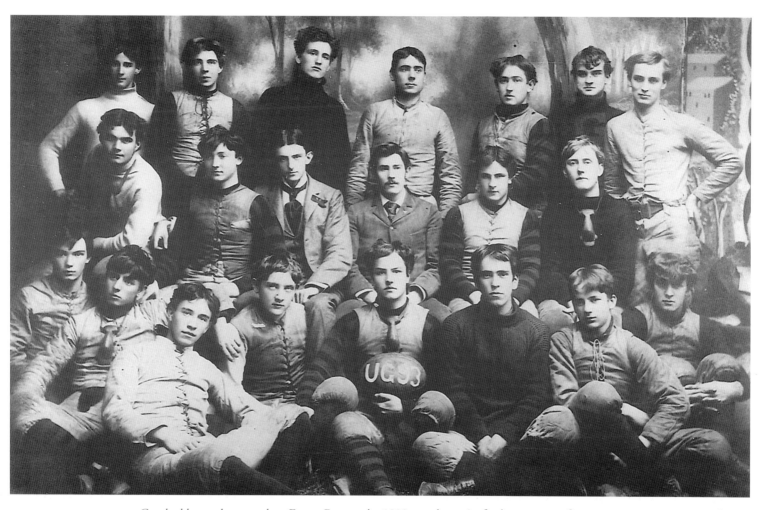

Coached by graduate student Ernest Brown, the 1893 squad won its final two games after a 0-2-1 start. Brown actually also played for the team at right halfback before suffering an injury in the second game against Vanderbilt. Early-style nose guards are visible in this image hanging from some of the players' necks.

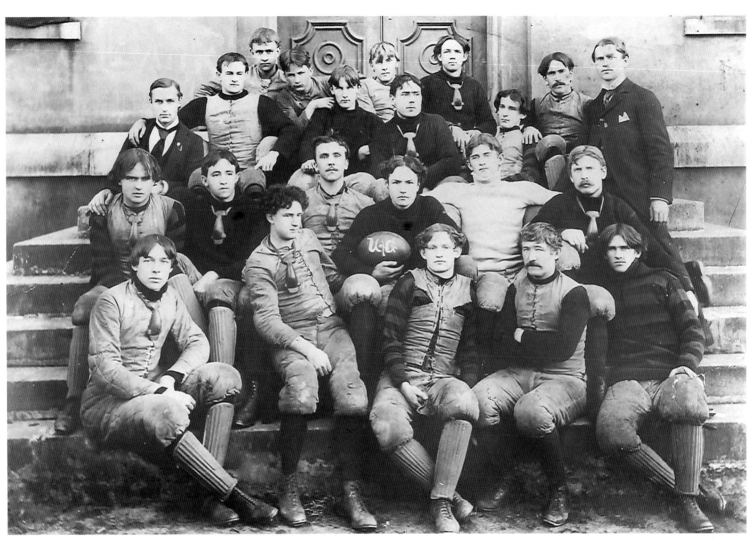

The 1894 team was the first to defeat rival Auburn. With the score tied late in the game, Rufus Nalley tackled an Auburn ball carrier in the end zone, scoring the winning safety in an eventual 10–8 win. The victors were awarded a silver cup presented from a four-horse carriage decorated with red and black ribbons. Five days later on Thanksgiving, Georgia defeated a Savannah athletic club to finish the season with a 5-1 record.

At only 24 years of age, Glenn "Pop" Warner began an illustrious, 44-year coaching career with a two-season stint at Georgia in 1895 and 1896. The "C" on Warner's sweater signifies his alma mater, Cornell University. In the early days of football, often a coach would represent his alma mater as Warner did, even though he was coaching at another school.

On October 30, 1897, fullback Richard Vonalbade Gammon was critically injured in a game against Virginia and died the following morning. Soon afterward, the Georgia General Assembly introduced a bill outlawing football at any school receiving state funds. The bill nearly passed before Gammon's mother, Rosalind, intervened, pleading that her son's death was no reason to abolish the sport of football—"the most cherished object of his life."

Located on the University of Georgia's North Campus, the Chapel bell has been rung by fans following each football victory for nearly 100 years. The longstanding tradition actually began after a 0–0 tie in 1901 against a heavily favored Auburn team.

Marvin Dickinson, a star halfback for Georgia from 1900 to 1902, became the Red and Black's head coach less than two weeks prior to the start of the 1903 season when Billy Reynolds abruptly left the position for a business opportunity in Canada. Only an assistant in 1904, Dickinson became the head coach again in 1905 and ended his two seasons as head coach with a 4-9 record.

The 1904 squad was coached by Charles Barnard, who had been an All-American at Harvard just three years before. In the season opener, playing the University of Florida (at the time, located in Lake City, Florida, not Gainesville) for the first time ever, Georgia triumphed 52–0 in Macon. The rest of the season was not nearly so successful—the team lost all five of its remaining games, scoring only 16 combined points.

One of the first prominent players at Georgia, Harold "War Eagle" Ketron lettered from 1901 to 1903, captaining the '03 squad which defeated Tennessee, Auburn, and Georgia Tech. Ketron, who it was said sometimes spit tobacco juice in his opponent's eye before making a tackle, returned to UGA to play again in 1906 after a two-season hiatus.

Georgia's first All-American was halfback Bob McWhorter, who was selected in 1913 by Parke Davis representing the *New York Herald*. When McWhorter arrived in 1910, he spearheaded the transformation of a sub-par football program into one of the very best in the South. McWhorter's 61 touchdowns would be a school record; however, they are not officially recognized, because of "insufficient documentation," which is true for most UGA football statistics prior to the late 1940s.

Only four years after playing at Vanderbilt, Alex Cunningham (see the Vanderbilt "V" on his sweater) became Georgia's head football coach in 1910 for $1,350 in salary. Before Cunningham, who would coach for 8 seasons, the team had 14 head coaches in its first 18 years, no one coaching for more than two campaigns. Of the nine individuals who have coached Georgia for at least 30 games, Cunningham's .679 winning percentage is third best.

In his initial season of 1912, Brooklyn, New York, native quarterback David Paddock teamed up with Bob McWhorter to form a dynamic rushing duo. Rushing for nearly 100 yards in a 20–0 victory over Georgia Tech, Paddock's performance was worthy of congratulations from baseball legend Ty Cobb following the game. Two years later, Paddock was captain of the team and a first team All-American despite missing one-third of the season.

Tackle Artie Pew was Georgia's first captain following the school's two-year suspension of football, during 1917-18 and the onset of World War I. In 1920, he was an All-Southern selection and duplicated the honor in 1921, along with being named All-American by the *Boston Post*. Georgia's primary placekicker from 1920 to 1921, Pew converted 48 extra points in his final two seasons.

Georgia's 1920 squad, captained by Ashel "Bum" Day (second row, holding ball), went undefeated, winning eight games and tying Virginia. The team scored a total of 250 points and allowed just 17, with 14 of those coming in a 21–14 win over Alabama. Georgia's nickname was the "Wildcats" at the beginning of the 1920 campaign, only to be changed to "Bulldogs" by *Atlanta Journal* writer Morgan Blake following the fifth game against Auburn.

Although Herman Stegeman was the head coach for just three seasons (1920–1922), his first team went undefeated and captured only the second S.I.A.A. title for Georgia in its first 27 seasons of playing football. Stegeman was also an accomplished basketball, baseball, and track coach at the school, winning championships in those three sports as well. Stegeman Coliseum, UGA's basketball arena, is named in his honor.

OFFICIAL
FOOTBALL
═ PROGRAM ═

BUM DAY
He Stopped Harvard at the Critical Moment

Georgia vs. Oglethorpe
Sat., Oct. 22, *1921*

UNIVERSITY OF GEORGIA ATHLETIC ASSOCIATION

Pictured is the program from the Georgia-Oglethorpe game of 1921, featuring Ashel "Bum" Day. After a 0–0 halftime score, the Bulldogs went on to defeat the Petrels, 14–0. Herman Stegeman did not play his starters, including Day, in the first half but did so following halftime. Day first enrolled at Georgia Tech and was an All-American in 1918. He then transferred to Georgia, where he was an All-Southern selection in 1920 and 1921.

Coach Herman Stegeman's 1921 Bulldogs were known for their defense, allowing only slightly more than 3 points, 5 first downs, and 137 yards per game during a 7-2-1 season. In contrast, offensively Georgia averaged 16, 14, and 284. Stegeman poses with the team here, second row from bottom, fourth from right.

A four-year starter from 1920 to 1923, Joe Bennett is still regarded as one of the greatest tackles ever to play for Georgia. Along with his superb blocking and tackling skills, he also had a knack for scoring unconventional touchdowns, recording three off blocked punts, one on a fumble recovery, and another by way of an interception return. Bennett also successfully kicked 11 extra points and 2 field goals.

A star quarterback and halfback at Georgia from 1907 to 1908 and 1910-12, George "Kid" Woodruff returned to UGA in 1923 as its head football coach. In five seasons, he compiled a 30-16-1 record, including a 9-1 mark in his final, 1927 season by the acclaimed "Dream and Wonder Team."

Starting all 10 of Georgia's games in 1927 at right end, Ivy "Chick" Shiver was named first team All-American by several selectors during a time when it was uncommon for southern players to be so recognized. Shiver was an exceptional pass receiver, blocker, and defender, and also served as the Bulldogs' backup punter. Three years following graduation, Shiver played major league baseball for Detroit and later for Cincinnati.

End Tom Nash was recognized by writer W. B. Hanna in 1927 as the greatest end in the country and player in the South. In Georgia's memorable 20–6 win over Alabama that season, Nash caught four passes for 75 yards and 2 touchdowns and intercepted a pass. Through the 2009 season, Georgia has had 23 first team consensus All-Americans. Nash was the first to earn the honor.

Glenn Lautzenhiser was the starting right tackle on the celebrated 1927 team. After the season, the junior from Atlanta was chosen All-Southern by two media outlets. In a banquet celebrating the season, an election was held to see who would captain Georgia's 1928 squad. Guard Roy Jacobson and Lautzenhiser tied with the same number of votes. The Bulldogs reportedly set a precedent that night for major college football teams by electing two captains.

Besides starting at center for the Bulldogs from 1927 to 1929, Joe Boland was recognized as one of the most accurate passers ever coached by Harry Mehre. Defensively, he was excellent at diagnosing opponents' plays, a hard tackler, and an outstanding pass defender. Boland, whose brother Kels and father Frank also played at Georgia, was the team's captain in 1929.

Ralph "Red" Maddox was one of "the Flaming Sophs" of 1929—a Bulldog team
where 8 of the 11 starters were just sophomores. Maddox was considered perhaps
the best "soph" of them all. By his senior season of 1931, Maddox had teamed with
another "flaming" redhead, Milton "Red" Leathers, for three years, giving Georgia
arguably the best guard tandem in the nation.

To the left is UGA's old Sanford Field, next to newly built Sanford Stadium to its right. Georgia played at Sanford Field from 1911 through the early portion of the 1929 season, compiling an impressive 50-11-4 record. For years following the construction of Sanford Stadium, Sanford Field was used as practice grounds.

An aerial view of Sanford Stadium during its dedication on October 12, 1929, is displayed. More than 30,000 spectators crammed into the stadium for Georgia's game against Yale. At the time, it was claimed to be the most hyped sporting event in the South during what was regarded as the greatest weekend in the city of Athens.

End Vernon "Catfish" Smith got his nickname in high school when he bit the head off a catfish after being dared by a classmate. As a sophomore at Georgia, he scored all the points in Sanford Stadium's inaugural game when the Bulldogs defeated Yale 15–0 in 1929. An All-Southern selection for three seasons (1929-31), Smith is one of 11 Georgia players currently belonging to the College Football Hall of Fame.

The hedges that surround the field at Sanford Stadium have been in place since the venue's inaugural game in 1929. The business manager for UGA's athletics, Charles E. Martin, initially preferred rose hedges after observing them at the 1926 Rose Bowl. However, when school horticulturalists suggested that roses would not thrive in the local climate, privet was planted instead.

A standout guard from 1933 to 1935, Frank Johnson was also a star forward on Georgia's basketball team. He accomplished what few have in collegiate athletics, earning all-conference honors in two sports. After being named first team All-SEC in football for 1935, Johnson was chosen for the All-SEC second team in basketball a few months later.

A sophomore guard in 1935, Pete Tinsley was moved to fullback the next season. However, because of Georgia's inadequate line play, he was moved back to guard midway through the 1936 campaign. The Bulldogs' monumental 7–7 tie with heavily favored Fordham and its "Seven Blocks of Granite" that season at New York's Polo Grounds was primarily owing to the spectacular performance of Tinsley. He was constantly in the Rams' backfield, smothering its touted running game.

Forrest "Spec" Towns, the greatest track and field legend in UGA history, won the gold medal in the 120-yard hurdles in record time during the 1936 Olympics in Berlin, Germany. Towns was also a reserve end on the 1936 and 1937 Georgia football teams. In a 47–7 loss to LSU in 1936, Towns scored the Bulldogs' lone touchdown when he picked up a blocked punt and sprinted 65 yards for a touchdown.

Bill Hartman was captain of the 1937 team and was considered by head coach Harry Mehre as the most valuable back he coached in his 10 years (1928–1937) at Georgia. Typically a fullback, Hartman was moved to quarterback late in his senior season because of team injuries and excelled at his new position. He was also an excellent punter and later a longtime assistant coach at the school.

Following four seasons as a Georgia assistant, Harry Mehre became the head
coach in 1928. His Bulldog teams chalked up a record of 59-34-6, including
6-2-2 against rival Georgia Tech and a combined 8-3 versus the eastern elite of
Yale and New York University. From 1938 to 1945, Mehre was the head coach
at Ole Miss, where he was 1-1-1 against his former Georgia team.

In the late 1930s, Quinton Lumpkin was recognized as one of the most outstanding athletes ever to compete for UGA. The 215-pound center from Macon, Georgia, captained the 1938 team and was an All-SEC selection for the second consecutive season. Immediately after his playing career, Lumpkin became an assistant at the school, coaching football, track, and freshman basketball for nearly 20 years.

Joel Hunt, a 31-year-old backfield coach at LSU and former Texas A&M three-time all-conference star, was named Georgia's head coach in January 1938, signing what he thought was a three-year contract. After a 5-1 start, Hunt's Bulldogs struggled down the stretch, finishing the season with a 5-4-1 record. In late December, Hunt was ousted from his position and replaced with one of his assistants—Wallace Butts.

Era of the Innovative "Little Round Man"

(1939–1960)

Georgia did not have to go too far to find its new head football coach for 1939, hiring an assistant from the previous staff, ends coach Wally Butts. Butts might have been inexperienced but he was familiar with Georgia, its people, its high school football, the university, and some powerful UGA alumni. With the new regime came many changes. Butts stocked the coaching staff with assistants he could rely on, including several former Bulldog players. The practices were long and rigorous, with time for few water breaks, if any at all. In addition, Georgia was going to employ a tactic fairly unique and rarely used by most teams at the time—a potent passing game.

After 5-6 and 5-4-1 records in Butts' first two seasons, the Bulldogs accomplished their best consecutive campaigns in history, winning 20 games in 1941 and 1942 combined, including the school's first two bowl contests. The '42 squad was replete with talented seniors, who had been freshmen in Butts' initial year, including Heisman Trophy winner Frank Sinkwich. As was the case with most other teams in the Southeast, World War II depleted the Bulldogs, leaving them primarily with 17-year-old freshmen too young for the war's draft. Georgia nearly decided to join most of the Southeastern Conference and sit out the 1943 season. Instead, the Bulldogs gallantly played on and somehow achieved a 13-7 combined record in 1943 and 1944. Led by the sensational Charley Trippi, Georgia won another 20 combined games in 1945 and 1946. Two years later, the Bulldogs seized their third conference title in seven seasons, proof that Georgia was becoming one of the best in college football during the decade. Evidently, however, all good things must come to an end.

Suddenly, from 1949 to 1958, Georgia football and its "Little Round Man"—the nickname for Butts because of his stocky build—went through an exhausting, losing stretch. Of the 10 seasons, only three were winning campaigns for Georgia and just once did it go to a bowl. The 1959 team did produce a diamond in the rough—an SEC title amid more than a decade of mostly lean years; however, this was followed by a mediocre 6-4 record. At the end of his twenty-second year as head coach, Butts decided it was time to step down.

In Columbus, Georgia, in 1939, Vassa Cate tries for a positive gain in a 7–0 loss to Auburn. Except for one meeting from 1916 to 1958, the Georgia-Auburn game was played each year at the neutral site of Columbus. Cate had one of the greatest punt returns in school history when his 37-yard, twisting return for a touchdown versus Tulane in 1937 proved to be the game winner in a 7–6 Georgia victory.

Halfback Heyward Allen was elected captain of the 1941 Bulldogs—the first Georgia team to earn a bowl invitation. Although he missed a good portion of the season due to a broken arm and was overshadowed by All-American Frank Sinkwich, Allen was responsible for nearly 700 total yards of offense, averaged 7 yards per rush, and scored 3 touchdowns rushing and passed for another three.

Frank Sinkwich broke his jaw in the second game of the 1941 season and played the rest of the year with a specially designed protector. Wearing the protective headgear, Sinkwich's performance in the 1942 Orange Bowl is still considered one of the best bowl performances of all time. In the 40-26 win over Texas Christian, "Fireball Frankie" passed for 243 yards, rushed for another 139, and was responsible for 4 touchdowns.

Known for his blazing speed, Lamar "Racehorse" Davis runs away from the opposition. From 1940 to 1942, Davis scored 24 touchdowns four different ways: 17 receiving, 3 rushing, 3 on punt returns, and 1 on a kick return. Against Centre College in 1941, Davis also scored a single point by retrieving a wild snap following a touchdown and running it in for the conversion. The two-point conversion play was not introduced by college football until 1958.

Sophomore halfback Charley Trippi (no. 62) had such a tremendous impact on Georgia's varsity during his initial season in 1942, senior superstar Frank Sinkwich (no. 21) was moved from halfback to fullback late in the year to make room for Trippi in the starting lineup.

Halfback-fullback Frank Sinkwich's 2,187 yards of total offense in 1942 led the nation and was the first time ever in college football that one player had surpassed 2,000 yards. After finishing fourth in the Heisman Trophy vote the year before, Sinkwich won the award in 1942. Of the trophy's first 24 recipients (1935–1958), he was the only player from a southeastern school to be so honored.

From Youngstown, Ohio, to UGA, to the Detroit Lions of the NFL, end George Poschner remained a teammate of the great Frank Sinkwich. Against third-ranked Alabama in 1942, Poschner caught two touchdown passes from Sinkwich, played a stellar defensive game, and was a primary reason for the Bulldogs' 21–10 win—one of the biggest victories in school history. Poschner would eventually be named first team All-American.

Starting right end Van Davis led the 1942 SEC and Rose Bowl champs in receiving, catching 33 passes for 455 yards. His number of receptions ranked fourth in the nation. Davis also scored four touchdowns that season—three receiving, one rushing—with three of those coming in the regular season's final game against Georgia Tech in a 34–0 win.

The 1942 Bulldogs are pictured in Southern California on their trip to Pasadena's Rose Bowl. Georgia defeated UCLA 9–0 to finish the season with an 11-1 record and was named national champions by several polls. It remains the only trip to the Rose Bowl in the football program's history.

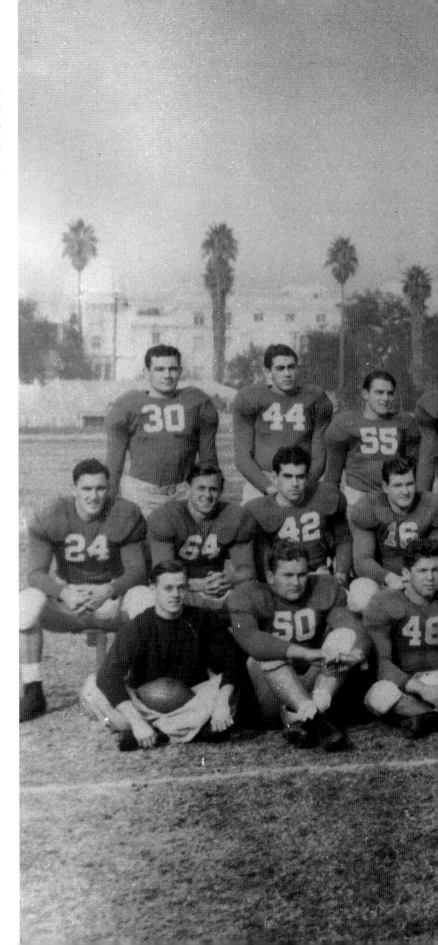

When World War I interrupted UGA football in 1917, Coach Alex Cunningham joined the U.S. Army. After returning to coach the team in 1919, he re-enlisted and attained the rank of general. Cunningham also served in World War II.

Harry "Koon" Kuniansky, a quick and rugged guard, was a regular on Georgia's winning bowl teams of 1941 and 1942. During his junior year, Kuniansky came down with appendicitis and later suffered a knee injury. Soon after the 1943 Rose Bowl, he was off to war and was wounded by a German air raid at Anzio, Italy. Lieutenant Kuniansky's wounds required nearly 100 stitches, confining him to a hospital bed for nearly a year.

An All-SEC guard in 1941 and 1942, Walter "Chief" Ruark saw action with the U.S. Infantry during World War II, beginning his service shortly following the 1943 Rose Bowl. On November 22, 1944, he was killed by enemy fire in Aachen, Germany. Whether playing football or serving the nation as a soldier, Ruark placed others before himself and was awarded both the Purple Heart and the Silver Star for bravery.

The demand for personnel able to defend the nation during World War II resulted in many football players entering military service. While Georgia's 1943 squad consisted primarily of 17-year-old freshmen too young for the draft, most other southeastern schools did not even field a team. These circumstances carried over into the next season. Freshman guard Herb St. John made the most of this opportunity and would earn the rare distinction of being named All-SEC for all four of his years (1944-47).

Guard-tackle Mike Castronis was captain of the inexperienced and war-depleted
Georgia team of 1943 that inexplicably achieved a 6-4 record. He was the first Bulldog
to be a three-time All-SEC selection (1943-45) and a first team All-American his senior
season. From 1947 until his death in 1987, Castronis, among other things, coached
high school football and was UGA's freshman football coach, cheerleader coach, and
assistant to the Dean of Men.

Visiting Athens for only the second time in 32 meetings, Alabama faces the fifth-ranked Bulldogs in 1946 and their extraordinary halfback Charley Trippi (no. 62). Trippi was responsible for 207 of Georgia's 249 total yards, rushing for 98 and passing for 109, and the game's two touchdowns in a 14–0 win by the Bulldogs.

The Bulldogs' potent backfield of 1946: right halfback John Donaldson (no. 31), fullback Dick McPhee (no. 63), quarterback John Rauch (no. 18), and left halfback Charley Trippi (no. 62). All but McPhee would play in the NFL and later become assistant coaches at Georgia.

Placekicker and reserve guard George Jernigan, nicknamed "Goat" or "the Springfield Rifle" (he was from Springfield, Tennessee), was considered the greatest kicker in football during Georgia's championship season of 1946. During a time when successfully kicking an extra point was far from a certainty, Jernigan made 47 of 52 attempts, or better than 90 percent. In comparison, all of college football that season made less than 66 percent.

Pictured are the starters on the 1946 squad, one of only three Georgia football teams to finish a season undefeated and untied. Nearly half the Bulldog starters—end Joe Tereshinski (first row, at far left), guard Herb St. John (first row, third from right), tackle Jack Bush (first row, second from right), quarterback John Rauch (second row, no. 18), and halfback Charley Trippi (second row, no. 62) earned some sort of All-SEC recognition.

Dan Edwards is running loose after catching a pass against the Clemson Tigers. An All-American in 1947, Edwards was on teams that defeated Clemson four consecutive seasons (1944-47). He caught touchdown passes as both a freshman and a sophomore against the Tigers. In this image, both teams are wearing dark-colored jerseys. It would not be until 1981 that the NCAA required one team to wear white jerseys in each game.

The 1948 Bulldogs finished the regular season with a 9-1 record, ranking eighth in the country before being upset by Texas in the Orange Bowl. Senior quarterback John Rauch (third row, no. 18) passed for 161 yards and a touchdown on 11 of 17 passing but it was not enough in a 41–28 loss to the Longhorns. It was only the eighth loss in 45 games for Rauch during his collegiate career.

Bernie Reid was the starting right guard and a co-captain of the 1948 SEC championship squad. Only three years after his final season at Georgia, Reid became head coach at Albany High School, winning more than 66 percent of his games in eight seasons. Later and for 25 years, he would scout for the Denver Broncos of the NFL.

Along with Bernie Reid, left end Weyman Sellers co-captained the 1948 Bulldogs. Although a fine college player, Sellers is primarily known for being one of the greatest high school football coaches ever in the state of Georgia. From 1952 to 1986, coaching several schools, Sellers won 223 games and captured two state championships at Athens High with two future UGA star quarterbacks—Fran Tarkenton in 1955 and Andy Johnson in 1969.

"Jarring" Johnny Rauch started his first game as a freshman quarterback in the season opener of 1945 against Murray State. Four years and 45 games later, he had not missed a start under center, finishing with a 36-8-1 record as a starter and throwing for 4,004 yards. Rauch's 36 victories was an NCAA record for 30 years; his passing total still ranks seventh-highest in school history.

A reserve his first three seasons, Joe Geri finally started as a senior in 1948 and the 24-year-old former Marine shined. The halfback from Phoenixville, Pennsylvania, led the Orange Bowl–bound Bulldogs in rushing and had a season-best 129 yards on 21 carries against Georgia Tech and its top-ranked rushing defense. Geri also scored 90 points that season on 9 touchdowns and 36 extra points.

Eli Maricich chose not to play football in high school but pursued the sport later when he was in the Marines. From 1946 to 1949, he was a do-everything kind of player for the Bulldogs, rushing and receiving the football, returning both kicks and punts, and excelling at defense. His eight interceptions in his junior year of 1948 led the nation, and the 189 return yards by way of the interceptions remain a single-season school record.

Tackle-guard Porter Payne, a star recruit from the Boys' High in Atlanta, lettered from 1946 to 1949. He was selected second team All-SEC as a junior and captain of the Bulldogs as a senior. During the Coach Butts era, the Bulldogs focused primarily on recruits from the Midwest. Of the 11 Bulldog starters in the 1949 Orange Bowl, Payne was the only one from the state of Georgia.

Holding for the place kick is Ken McCall (no. 23), a versatile player who excelled in all three facets of the game: offense, defense, and special teams. As a freshman in 1944, McCall shared the quarterback duties, throwing for four touchdowns, rushing for one, and returning an interception for another. After two years in the military, he returned to Georgia and tallied 686 punt return yards and 10 interceptions from 1947 to 1949.

Since the late 1940s, Dan Magill has held myriad positions with the University's athletic department, including secretary of the Georgia Bulldog Club, Assistant Athletic Director, and Sports Information Director. From 1955 to 1988, he coached the school's tennis team, retiring as the NCAA's winningest tennis coach of all time. Located on campus, the Dan Magill Tennis Complex is named in his honor. Magill is also recognized as the foremost historian regarding University of Georgia athletics.

Halfback Billy Mixon became a part of Bulldog lore on a Friday night in Athens in 1949. "The Tifton Tornado" scored the game-winning touchdown against LSU on a one-yard dive. A year later, Mixon's 705 rushing yards would stand for 20 years as the fourth highest at Georgia for a single season, only behind totals tallied by All-Americans Frank Sinkwich and Charley Trippi.

Left to right, assistants Ralph Jordan, Bill Hartman, and Sterling Dupree gather with head coach Wally Butts and his dog Rip during the 1950 season. "Shug" Jordan would become the head coach at Auburn the following year, coaching the Tigers through 1975. The 1950 Bulldogs opened their season defeating 15th-ranked Maryland en route to a 6-2-3 regular-season record and Presidential Cup appearance.

Linebacker Art Decarlo, a native of Youngstown, Ohio, unofficially recovered eight fumbles in the first four games of the 1950 season—the first four games Decarlo played on Georgia's varsity. Currently, the school record for fumble recoveries—a statistic only officially kept since the 1979 season—is eight for an *entire* career. Because of numerous personnel changes by Coach Wally Butts, Decarlo played five different positions during the 1952 season. A sophomore All-SEC linebacker in 1950, Decarlo received all-conference honors at defensive back as a senior. During the '52 campaign, Georgia's jack-of-all-trades intercepted 3 passes from his safety position and caught 18 passes for 317 yards and 3 touchdowns at end.

From 1947 to 1950, end Bobby Walston caught 57 passes for 1,183 yards and 11 touchdowns. His nearly 21-yards-per-catch average is a school record for those with at least 40 career receptions. Walston never kicked a field goal while at Georgia but made 80 in 12 seasons with the Philadelphia Eagles. During his NFL career, he also kicked 365 extra points, caught 311 passes, and scored 46 touchdowns from his end position.

On November 25, 1950, halfback Zippy Morocco scored three touchdowns against Furman in a 40–0 victory in Athens. Only an estimated 1,000 spectators witnessed the game, because of chilling, eight-degree weather. Two weeks later against Texas A&M in the Presidential Cup, the junior from Youngstown, Ohio, was at it again, scoring on a 30-yard rush and a 65-yard punt return. Morocco also became the school's first All-American in basketball (1953).

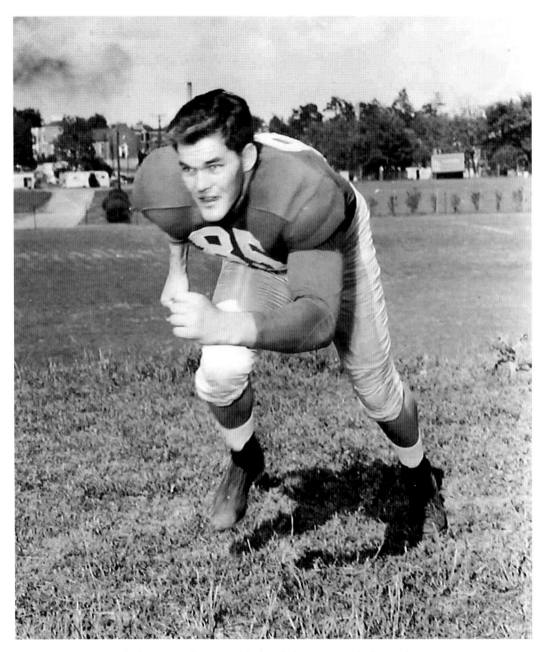

Francis Marion Campbell was an All-SEC tackle for all three seasons he lettered at Georgia (1949-51). He would later star in the NFL, was a head coach in the league for nine seasons, and returned to Athens in 1994 as Georgia's defensive coordinator for one season. Born in Chester, South Carolina, Campbell got his name and nickname from General Francis Marion, the "Swamp Fox"—a Revolutionary War hero from South Carolina.

Against Auburn in 1951, junior Lauren Hargrove rushed for a career-high 167 yards on 14 carries in a 46–14 win by the Bulldogs. Hargrove's yardage and the team's 447 rushing yards would be Georgia single-game bests for more than 20 years. Auburn's second and final touchdown was a 35-yard scoring pass by its backup quarterback and future Bulldog head coach, sophomore Vince Dooley.

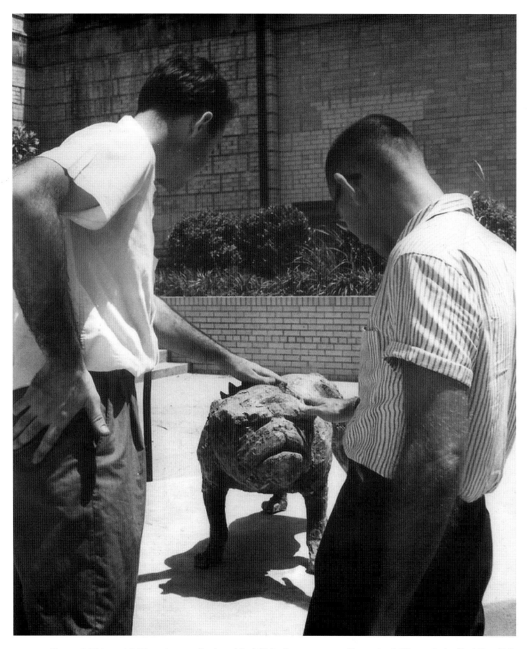

From 1951 to 1955, prior to the heralded "Uga" mascots at Georgia, Mike, a brindled English bulldog, was the school's mascot. As shown here, a bronze statue of Mike is located at the entrance of the university's Memorial Hall. The statue was cast as a master's thesis by student Gene Owens of Fort Worth, Texas.

After making 80 career receptions at Georgia (1950-52), a team record for nearly two decades, end Harry Babcock was the first overall pick of the 1953 NFL Draft, selected by San Francisco. To date, Babcock is one of four Bulldogs chosen first in the draft. The other three are Frank Sinkwich (1943), Charley Trippi (1945), and Matt Stafford (2009).

In the season-opening game of 1952, sophomore Jimmy Campagna, the "Rochester Rocket," returned a punt 100 yards for a touchdown against Vanderbilt. Later in the year, he carried a 60-yard punt return for a touchdown versus Penn and a 96-yard kickoff return for a score against Auburn. Campagna's 18.0 career punt-return average from 1951 to 1954 is a Georgia record for those with at least 10 returns.

On November 21, 1953, senior quarterback Zeke Bratkowski completed a 15-yard pass to Harold Pilgrim late in a game against Mississippi Southern, breaking the NCAA record for most passing yards in a career. Bratkowski, who passed for 4,863 yards while at Georgia, was also an accomplished punter, leading the nation in punting with a 42.6 average in 1953.

John Carson is the University of Georgia's most recent four-letter athlete, lettering in football, basketball, baseball, and golf. He is one of only two Bulldogs ever to lead the country in receiving, ranking first in 1953 with 45 catches for 663 yards. A first team All-American that season, Carson would play seven years of pro football, making the Pro Bowl in 1957.

Wally Butts compiled a 140-86-9 overall record, including 5-2-1 in bowl games, in his 22 seasons (1939–1960) as head coach. During an era of primarily run-oriented offenses, Butts was known for his innovative passing game. Ten of his teams from 1940 to 1953 ranked in the nation's top 10 in passing.

Bob Clemens, a large, 200-pound fullback, was nicknamed "Foots" because of his size 14 shoe. As a sophomore in 1952 and junior in 1953, he led the Bulldogs in rushing with more than 450 yards each season on pass-oriented teams. Clemens' 1,297 rushing yards from 1952 to 1954 ranked in Georgia's top five for a career until the mid-1970s.

After leading the team in rushing, kickoff returns, and punting as a junior in 1954, fullback Bobby Garrard, an All-SEC selection, was named captain for his senior campaign. As a Bulldog, Garrard ranked third at Georgia in rushing during the decade of the 1950s and also intercepted seven passes on defense, returning one against North Carolina in 1955 for a 51-yard touchdown.

An all-state halfback at Columbus High in Columbus, Georgia, Knox Culpepper was immediately shifted to fullback when he arrived at UGA in 1952. To utilize Culpepper's speed, the Georgia coaching staff had him return kicks all three seasons he earned a varsity letter (1954-56). Culpepper was named captain of the team in 1956.

During a pre-game party before the home opener of 1956 against Florida State in Athens, Sonny and Cecelia Seiler were urged by friends to escort their white English bulldog to the game. "We never intended to take Uga to Sanford Stadium that day," said Sonny. In the stands, Uga caused so much excitement that, soon afterward, he was selected to be the school's mascot.

From 1955 to 1957, Ken Cooper was a standout end, punter, and the team's primary placekicker, converting 24 extra points and kicking 3 field goals. His 36-yard field goal against Florida State in 1956 was a game winner in a 3–0 victory and was the longest ever kicked at Sanford Stadium to that time. His conversion following a bad snap in a game against Texas a season later, remains Georgia's last score resulting from a dropkick.

From his halfback position, Jimmy Orr led the SEC in receiving in 1955 and 1957 on teams that averaged only five pass completions per game. Named the NFL's 1958 offensive rookie of the year with Pittsburgh, Orr was considered one of the greatest receivers in the league during the 1960s, playing for the Steelers and Colts.

Diminutive halfback J. B. Davis, weighing all of 155 pounds, was captain
of the 1957 Bulldog squad. The season before as a junior, Davis ran back a
punt 58 yards for a touchdown in a 7–7 tie against the heavily favored Miami
Hurricanes. Two weeks later against Alabama in Birmingham, his 80-yard punt
return for a touchdown was the difference in a 16–13 Georgia victory.

Quarterback Charley Britt (no. 17) signals a touchdown as fullback Theron Sapp (no. 40) stumbles into the end zone against Georgia Tech in 1957. Sapp's touchdown came on fourth down from the Yellow Jackets' one-yard line, breaking a scoreless tie late in the third quarter and proving eventually to end an eight-game winning streak by Georgia Tech over Georgia. Forever known as the "Drought-Breaker," Sapp was honored in 1959 when jersey number 40 was retired.

Growing up in Blythe, Georgia, three Dye brothers left their family farm for Athens to attend and play football at UGA during the 1950s. First, there was Wayne, followed by Nat (no. 79), and finally the youngest, Pat (no. 60).

Right tackle Nat Dye received All-SEC recognition in his final two seasons of 1957 and 1958.

Charley Britt remains one of the last outstanding all-around players at Georgia, excelling in all phases of the game. The starting quarterback from 1957 to 1959, Britt passed for 1,281 career yards and rushed for another 539. He also averaged nearly 12 yards per punt return and intercepted 8 passes, including one he returned 100 yards for a touchdown against Florida in 1959.

In April 1959, Don Soberdash was elected captain of the Bulldogs for that upcoming season. Concerned about many of the players being overweight, the senior halfback asserted that if anyone returned to fall practice too heavy "there would be head knocking." No one showed up overweight. The Bulldogs, who had a 4-6 record in 1958, won the SEC title and finished with a 10-1 mark.

Don Leebern followed his father's path, attending and playing football at UGA. As part of the 1959 championship team, he started 9 of the Bulldogs' 10 regular-season games at right tackle. Today, he is a member of the Board of Regents.

After leading the unbeaten freshman squad of 1957 in rushing, fullback Bill Godfrey was held out the following season. In his first varsity contest, "Tater-Bug" scored on a spectacular, 40-yard jaunt against Alabama, a decisive play in the 17–3 win over the Crimson Tide. Of the 15 players on the 1959 SEC title team to start at least one game, Godfrey, who led the Bulldogs in rushing, was the lone underclassman.

Jimmy Vickers was an outstanding player and coach at Georgia. The starting left end from 1957 to 1959, he was one of only two Bulldogs named to both the AP and UPI All-SEC first team in 1959. A Georgia assistant from 1971 to 1976, Vickers coached five first-team All-American offensive linemen, three of whom were consensus All-Americans, before becoming the offensive coordinator at Ole Miss in 1977.

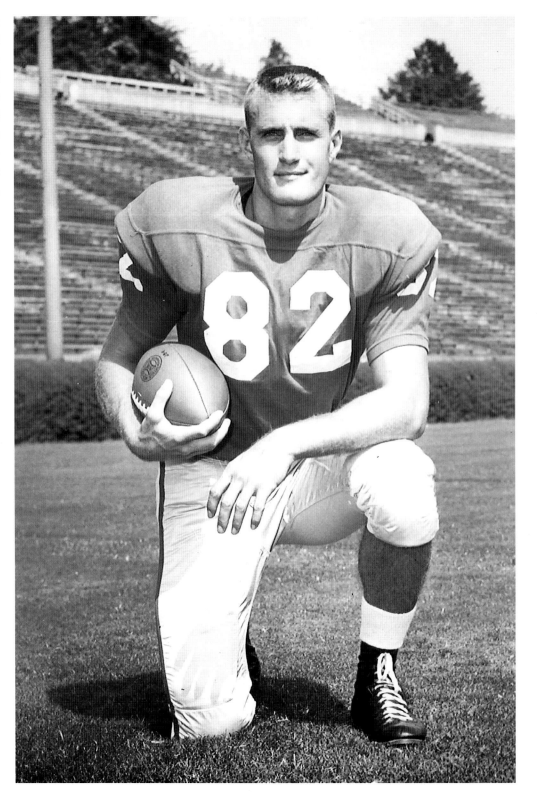

Bill Herron was a highly touted end from Sanger, California, and a junior college All-American. He played at Georgia in 1958 and 1959, but injuries persisted throughout his collegiate career, restricting him to only 15 catches. Nevertheless, Herron made one of the biggest receptions in Bulldog history, catching a fourth-down pass from Fran Tarkenton for a touchdown, with only seconds remaining in the game, to defeat Auburn in 1959 for the SEC championship.

Halfback Fred Brown, whose father and three uncles all played at Alabama, led the SEC in rushing yards per attempt (6.6) as a sophomore in 1958 and receptions (31) as a senior in 1960. The 2,133 career all-purpose yards amassed by "Flyin' Fred" ranked third all time at Georgia upon his graduation, only behind greats Frank Sinkwich and Charley Trippi.

In 1960, quarterback Fran Tarkenton ended his senior season first in the SEC and tied for fifth in the nation in passing. He would have a spectacular, 18-season NFL career with the Vikings and Giants, holding several league passing records upon his retirement. Tarkenton has been inducted into both the College Football and Pro Football Halls of Fame.

Pat (no. 60) and Nat Dye (no. 79) were both alternate captains during their senior seasons, Nat in 1958 and Pat in 1960. Pat almost decided to attend Georgia Tech instead of following his brother to Georgia. When he spurned Tech, Pat was told by a Yellow Jacket coach he'd never defeat Tech as a Bulldog. As a player, Pat was a perfect 4-0 versus the Yellow Jackets and 7-0 as a head coach at Auburn from 1981 to 1992.

Pictured is Georgia's lethal kicking pair of the late 1950s and early 1960s. Placekicker Durward Pennington (no. 15) ranked fourth in 1959 and third in 1960 in kick scoring for the entire nation. Punter-halfback Bobby Walden (no. 39) ranked first in the country in punting for 1958 and was second in 1960. Both went on to kick in the professional ranks with Walden becoming one of the greatest punters in NFL history.

Pressure is applied to Georgia Tech quarterback Stan Gann (no. 12) by Georgia tackle Bobby Green (no. 74) during the 1960 Bulldogs–Yellow Jackets game in Athens. Georgia's defense held Gann and company to just 254 yards of total offense in the Bulldogs' thrilling 7–6 victory. The game marked the first time brothers had opposed each other in the series—guard Wally Williamson for Georgia and halfback Billy Williamson for Tech.

Guard Pat Dye had a prominent career as a Bulldog, which ended in fine fashion against Georgia Tech in 1960. In what was also Coach Wally Butts' final game at Georgia, Dye blocked an extra point attempt of Tommy Wells in the first half, which proved to be the difference in a one-point Bulldog win. From 1954 to 1960, whether it was Wayne, Nat, or Pat, a Dye brother played in seven Georgia–Georgia Tech games a combined nine times.

Coach Wally Butts proudly hoists a trophy his Bulldogs won. In Butts' 22 years as head coach, Georgia was victorious in five bowl games and captured four SEC championships.

VINCE WHO?

(1961–1970)

Johnny Griffith, a former Georgia player and an assistant the previous five seasons, was the successor to Coach Wally Butts. Griffith lasted only three years, compiling a disappointing 10-16-4 record, including 1-8 against the Bulldogs' "big three" of Florida, Auburn, and Georgia Tech.

In December 1963, Joel Eaves, UGA's new athletic director, hired one of his former pupils to lead the school's floundering football program. Whereas most Bulldog followers expected an experienced, well-known coach, Eaves appointed 31-year-old Vince Dooley—a former football and basketball player under Eaves at Auburn, the Tigers' freshman football coach from 1961 to 1963, and, for the most part, a complete and utter unknown. A comment by Lynn Hughes, Dooley's leading passer in 1964, was typical of player reaction. Hughes said years later, "[Some teammates and I] were sitting on the steps at Stegeman (home of UGA's athletic and physical education departments) wondering, 'Who the hell is Vince Dooley?'" It did not take long for the young coach to become familiar to Georgia supporters as he guided his first group of Bulldogs to an astounding 7-3-1 record. Dooley also received the school's first bowl invitation in five years and was named the United Press International's SEC coach of the year.

From the outset, Dooley exhibited outstanding organizational skills and assembled an excellent group of assistants. The only other thing the football program at the University of Georgia had needed to be successful was a handful of talented players, who apparently were already in place. Among these talents were Hughes, George Patton, and Edgar Chandler, who helped bring Georgia an SEC championship in only Dooley's third year. Two seasons later in 1968, standouts like Jake Scott, Bill Stanfill, and Billy Payne were primary contributors to the Bulldogs winning their second conference title in three campaigns, a feat that had not been accomplished in 20 years since the pinnacle of the Coach Butts era.

Just as rapidly as Dooley had turned the program around, it began to show new signs of mediocrity as the Bulldogs slumped to 5-5-1 and 5-5 records in 1969 and 1970, respectively. It was becoming evident that to compete in the rugged SEC and with their intrastate rival Georgia Tech, who had defeated the Bulldogs in both 1969 and 1970, traditional approaches to recruitment had to be rethought.

Pete Case, the 1957 Georgia High School Class AAA lineman of the year, followed his older brother Bud to UGA from Decatur, Georgia. An extremely quick lineman, Case started at left tackle for the Bulldogs in 1960 and 1961 and was the team's captain as a senior.

Larry Rakestraw was Georgia's leading passer for three consecutive seasons (1961-63), passing for a career total of 3,142 yards. Against the Miami Hurricanes in 1963, the senior quarterback broke the NCAA's single-game record for passing yards with 407 in a 31–14 win. Rakestraw's passing yardage versus the Hurricanes remained a school record for 30 years.

Johnny Griffith made the most of the one season he lettered at Georgia, scoring on an 89-yard run against Furman in 1946. His run remains tied for first for the longest rush in school history. From 1956 to 1960, Griffith served as an assistant coach, until being named the Bulldogs' 21st head coach in 1961. His head coaching reign lasted only three seasons, recording just a 10-16-4 mark.

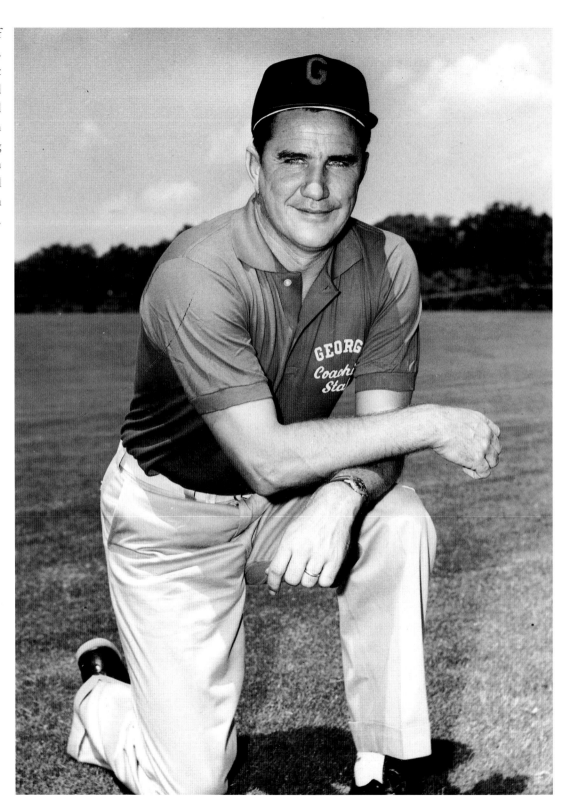

"Big Jim" Wilson, from Pittsburgh, Pennsylvania, stood at 6-foot-3 and weighed 245 pounds—the heaviest starter on the 1964 team by 20 pounds. Coach Vince Dooley once described him as "the strongest player I've ever seen."

Placekicker Bob Etter's 134 points from 1964 to 1966 ranked sixth all time at Georgia and first among placekickers upon his departure from the school. Etter successfully made 25 of 35 field goals and 53 of 56 extra points. He also remains the last Bulldog kicker to score a touchdown. When a field goal attempt was botched, Etter scooped up the ball and ran for the game-winning score in a 14–7 victory over Florida in 1964.

Tackle Ray Rissmiller, from Easton, Pennsylvania, chose Georgia in 1961 over 44 other scholarship offers because reportedly he liked the warm weather. He was one of two first team All-Americans on the 1964 team. Rissmiller was eventually selected 20th overall in the 1965 NFL draft and played for three teams in three seasons in the pros.

On a soggy field at Sanford Stadium, Preston Ridlehuber fights for yardage against Georgia Tech in 1964. In a game where the Bulldogs and Yellow Jackets combined to fumble 8 times and gain just 325 total yards, the junior quarterback scored the contest's only touchdown on a three-yard option run. Ridlehuber, who was moved to halfback during his senior season, would play three seasons in professional football as a running back.

Quarterback Lynn Hughes led the Bulldogs in passing in his first varsity season of 1964. The following year, he was moved to safety, but occasionally saw spot duty at his original position during the 1965 and 1966 seasons. While at Georgia, Hughes passed for 712 yards, rushed for 188, and was responsible for 8 touchdowns.

In a 24–10 win over Vanderbilt in 1965, "Bullet" Bob Taylor rushes for some of his 88 yards on 19 carries. Through the first four games of the '65 season with the senior halfback as its primary rusher, Georgia went undefeated and ranked fifth in the nation. After a season-ending injury to Taylor against Florida State in the fifth game, the Bulldogs won just two of their final six contests.

Following a fine career at Georgia, where he caught 54 passes for 769 yards from 1963 to 1965 and was an all-conference selection as both a sophomore and senior, end Pat Hodgson played one season in the NFL with the Washington Redskins. He returned to UGA in 1972 to coach quarterbacks and receivers through the 1977 season.

At UGA's Homecoming 1966, what was to become a long-standing tradition began with the passing of a dog collar from one Uga mascot to his successor. Uga I had been the mascot for more than 10 years and had begun showing signs of age. With most of the 45,348 spectators in Sanford Stadium chanting Uga's praises, his 11-month-old son became Georgia's Uga II.

Fullback Ronnie Jenkins runs up the middle against Florida in 1966. Trailing 10–3 at halftime, Georgia scored 24 unanswered points to upset the seventh-ranked Gators and their eventual Heisman Trophy–winning quarterback, Steve Spurrier. Jenkins rushed for 88 yards on 20 carries, including a three-yard scoring run early in the third quarter, which began the Bulldogs' memorable comeback.

George Patton, a two-time All-American who finished 10th in the Heisman Trophy balloting in 1966, is arguably the greatest defensive lineman in Georgia football history. In his final game as a Bulldog, Patton was inserted at quarterback late in the 1966 Cotton Bowl against Southern Methodist University. A quarterback in high school, Patton was appearing at the position for the first time since his arrival at UGA.

End Dennis Hughes earned first team All-SEC recognition as a junior in 1968 when he had 491 receiving yards, including 100-yard games against Clemson (128) and Ole Miss (134). Hughes' 1,207 career receiving yards from 1967 to 1969 was a school record upon his graduation.

Hailing from Cedartown, Georgia, offensive tackle Edgar Chandler was a member of Coach Vince Dooley's first recruiting class of 1964. Chandler was considered faster than some of the backs he blocked for during his Bulldog career. He was recognized as a first team All-American in 1966 and 1967 and played on the defensive side of the ball as a middle linebacker in professional football from 1968 to 1973.

As a junior, cornerback Terry Sellers led the 1966 SEC champs with five interceptions. The following season, having previously never returned a punt at Georgia, Sellers returned 15 punts for 203 yards, including a 62-yard touchdown against Virginia Military Institute. His 13.5 punt return average remains ranked in the school's top ten for best in a season.

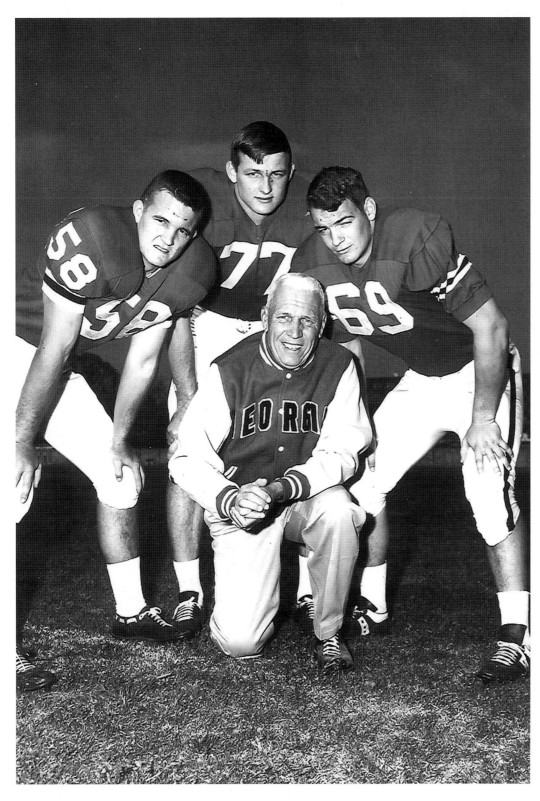

Linebacker Tommy Lawhorne (no. 58), defensive tackle Bill Stanfill (no. 77), and defensive guard Tim Callaway (no. 69) pose with the team's director of recruiting, Sterling Dupree, in 1967. Dupree, who in his younger years was occasionally misidentified as film star Humphrey Bogart, was an assistant at Georgia for 24 seasons. He also coached at South Carolina, Florida, and his alma mater of Auburn, and served as an officer in World War II under General George Patton.

Defensive coordinator Erk Russell instructs members of his 1967 defense, including future All-Americans Bill Stanfill (no. 77) and Steve Greer (no. 60). Defensively in 1967, the Bulldogs yielded just 10.5 points and 212.6 yards per game. They ranked fifth in the nation in passing defense.

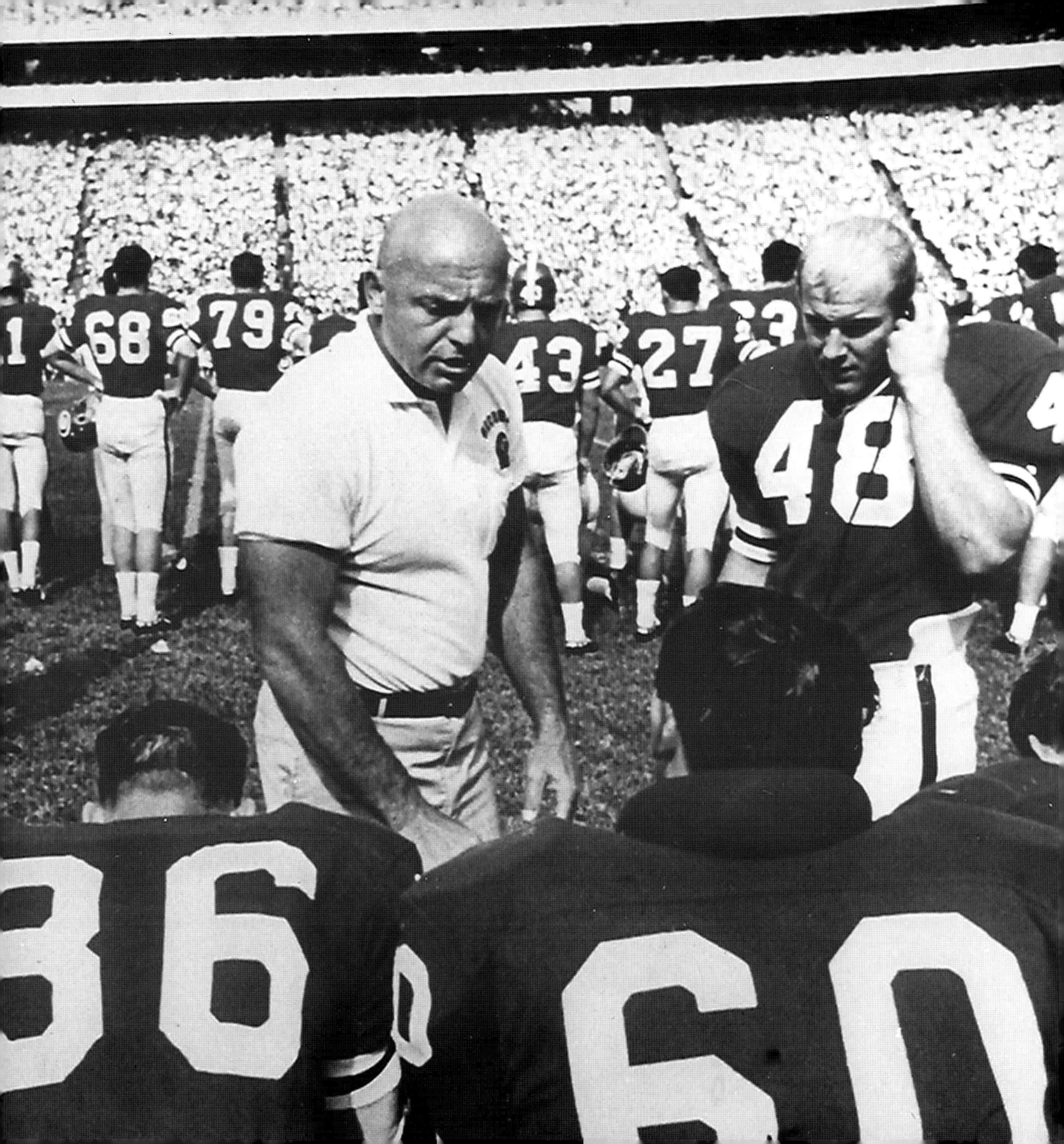
68
79
43
27
48

Kirby Moore was one of the first of a long line of outstanding running quarterbacks during the Coach Vince Dooley era. The Dothan, Alabama, native also led Georgia in passing from 1965 to 1967. Moore is one of only two Bulldog quarterbacks in history to pass for at least 1,700 yards and rush for 1,000.

The 1968 Bulldogs ended their regular season with an undefeated 8-0-2 mark and ranked fourth in the nation. Standing in the middle of the team dressed in white is head coach Vince Dooley, who captured his second SEC title that season in just five seasons at Georgia and at only 36 years of age.

Decades prior to playing a key role in bringing the 1996 Olympics to Atlanta and becoming chairman of the Augusta National Golf Club, home of the Masters, in 2006, Billy Payne was a standout on offense and defense for the Bulldogs. In 1966 and 1967, he was a starting offensive end, catching a combined 22 passes. Switching to defensive end as a senior, Payne intercepted three passes and was named first team All-SEC.

Robert "Happy" Dicks was an excellent tackler, who was also outstanding at defending the pass from his linebacker position. On Georgia's SEC title team of 1966, Dicks ranked second with four interceptions as a sophomore. For the next two seasons, he started for the Bulldogs, earning second team All-SEC honors in 1968.

Following in the footsteps of his brother Bill, who was Georgia's primary placekicker in 1962 and 1963, Macon, Georgia, native Jim McCullough led the Bulldogs in scoring from 1967 to 1969, kicking 84 extra points and 22 field goals.

Defensive tackle Bill Stanfill was the only underclassman on the starting defense of Georgia's 1966 SEC title team. He was named second team All-SEC that year and would earn first team status as a junior and senior. In 1968, playing on another SEC championship squad, Stanfill won the Outland Trophy, given annually to college football's best interior lineman. He remains the only Bulldog to win the coveted award.

Although he played for only two seasons (1967 and 1968) on Georgia's varsity, safety Jake Scott still holds the school record for career interceptions (16) and touchdowns scored on returns (4). Scott also had one of the best NFL careers by a Bulldog, intercepting 49 passes for Miami and Washington in nine seasons from 1970 to 1978.

Bulldog cheerleaders root for the team during the 1960s. According to the university, a cheerleader first appeared at the school's inaugural game. Bob Gantt is identified as one who urged the Red and Black fans to support the squad during Georgia's 50–0 victory against Mercer in 1892. Gantt, from Athens, also brought the team's first mascot to the game—a goat.

As only a sophomore, Mike Cavan quarterbacked Georgia to an undefeated regular season in 1968, an SEC championship, and a trip to the Sugar Bowl. He was recognized as the conference's Sophomore of the Year. Cavan's 1,619 passing yards stood as the second most in school history for a single season until 1991. Cavan would become a Bulldog assistant in 1977, coaching running backs for nine seasons.

Defensive guard Steve Greer was one of just two underclassmen starters on Georgia's 1967 defense. Two seasons later as a senior, he was recognized as a first team All-American. Greer was an assistant coach for the Bulldogs from 1979 to 1993.

Georgia cheerleaders lead the team onto the field during the late 1960s. In 1970, the Cheerleaders Alumni Association was organized, and former spirit leaders were invited to the school's Homecoming football game to cheer on the Bulldogs.

Peter Rajecki, a native of Gelsenkirchen-Buer, Germany, was Georgia's first soccer-styled placekicker. From 1968 to 1970, he was the team's main kickoff man and made two field goals during his career, including a then school-record 54-yarder against Mississippi State in 1970. Holding for Rajecki is Sam Mrvos, a longtime assistant coach and Georgia's placekicker from 1951 to 1953.

He did not have the greatest speed, but Charlie Whittemore had other skills and intangibles, which allowed him to become one of the greatest receivers ever at Georgia. From 1968 to 1970, his 114 catches for 1,680 yards were both school records until they were broken by Lindsay Scott in 1981. Whittemore coached Bulldog tight ends and receivers, including Scott, for 13 seasons from 1978 to 1990.

Tommy Lyons excelled both on the gridiron and in the classroom. He anchored Georgia's offensive line as its starting center from 1968 to 1970, earning All-SEC honors his senior season. Lyons also received a National Football Foundation Scholar-Athlete Award in 1970 and an NCAA Post-Graduate Scholarship a year later.

THE BUMPY ROAD TO PERFECTION

(1971–1980)

During the University of Georgia's Christmas holidays of 1970, a long overdue change was implemented that would in time alter the face of the school's football program substantially. The first African-American players were signed; four of the five recruits would experience their first varsity action in September 1972. Although they had been attempting to sign black players for years, the Bulldogs were among the last in the SEC to play them, along with LSU and Ole Miss.

In 1971 and for only the third time in history, Georgia won 11 games. In 1972, the NCAA allowed freshmen to play varsity football for the first time since the Korean War. The ruling received mixed reviews at Georgia, but soon thereafter, very few disapproved. During the 1973 campaign and amid consecutive seven-win seasons, "Dump Dooley" bumper stickers began to crop up. Following a 6-6 record in 1974, those sentiments spread. It was the lowest point of the Coach Vince Dooley era and especially disheartening for defensive coordinator Erk Russell, whose defensive unit had unexpectedly faltered in 1974 after years of excellence. Just prior to the 1975 season, Russell labeled his defense the "Junkyard Dogs" for motivational purposes—the unit was small and inexperienced but quick and mean. Georgia was projected to finish toward the bottom of the SEC that season but nearly won the conference title. The Bulldogs captured Dooley's third conference championship in 1976, with the subsequent year being the coach's only losing season while at Georgia. It was assumed that the 1978 campaign would be another losing one, but the "Wonderdogs" instead recorded a 9-1-1 regular-season mark.

Georgia ended the turbulent '70s on a down note, winning only six games in 1979. Like 10 years before, the Bulldogs were a talented but not a complete team. As it looked forward to a new decade, Georgia's missing piece was a top-notch running back. Never before had there been a college football player who combined the power, speed, and explosiveness possessed by tailback Herschel Walker. Nine years earlier, Herschel would not have been playing for Georgia; he was black and a freshman. Nevertheless, in 1980, he along with a group of overachieving Bulldogs (the team was 42 percent African-American that year) achieved a 12-0 perfect record and the school's first uncontestable national championship.

In early December 1970, Chuck Kinnebrew and Larry West became the first two African-American football recruits to sign at Georgia. Three additional blacks would sign soon after. Kinnebrew, from Rome, Georgia, would eventually start as a defensive right guard on the 1974 team.

Along with Horace King, Larry West, Chuck Kinnebrew, and Richard Appleby, Clarence Pope was among the first group of African-American recruits signed to play football at UGA. Pope started as a linebacker for the Bulldogs in 1973.

Cornerback Larry West was primarily a two-year reserve until starting for the Bulldogs in 1974. From 1972 to 1974, he intercepted six passes, including one thrown by Vanderbilt's Steve Lainhart that West returned 75 yards for a touchdown in 1972.

A hometown product of Athens, Horace King made a big splash his first year at UGA, rushing for a record 829 yards, including 291 against Florida, in only five games on Georgia's freshman Bullpups team of 1971 (the old record was 397 yards). During his varsity career (1972-74), the senior All-SEC selection totaled more than 2,000 yards of all-purpose yardage and 20 touchdowns. King played nine seasons in the NFL with Detroit.

Approximately three decades after they were first introduced at Georgia, female cheerleaders root for the team. Following many years of student attempts to persuade UGA officials, female football cheerleaders made their first appearance at a game on October 12, 1940, against Ole Miss.

Buzy Rosenberg breaks would-be tacklers on a punt return against Oregon State in the 1971 season opener. In the 56–25 victory, the junior from Atlanta returned five punts for 202 yards, including returns of 79 and 56 yards for touchdowns. Rosenberg's total return yardage and two returns for scores against the Beavers remain single-game school records.

In 1970 and 1971, flanker Jimmy Shirer had the rare distinction of being both one of the top receivers for the Bulldogs and the team's punter. He is mostly remembered for the 12-yard reception he made against Georgia Tech in 1971, when he barely stayed in bounds, leading to the winning touchdown with only seconds remaining.

In 1971, defensive coordinator Erk Russell (right) takes notes while sophomore Jerone Jackson (no. 13) looks on. Jackson, an occasional starter at cornerback that season, would eventually become Georgia's starting free safety in 1972 and 1973. Russell had already established himself as one of college football's most distinguished assistant coaches and would depart UGA 10 years later as likely the most celebrated Bulldog assistant in history.

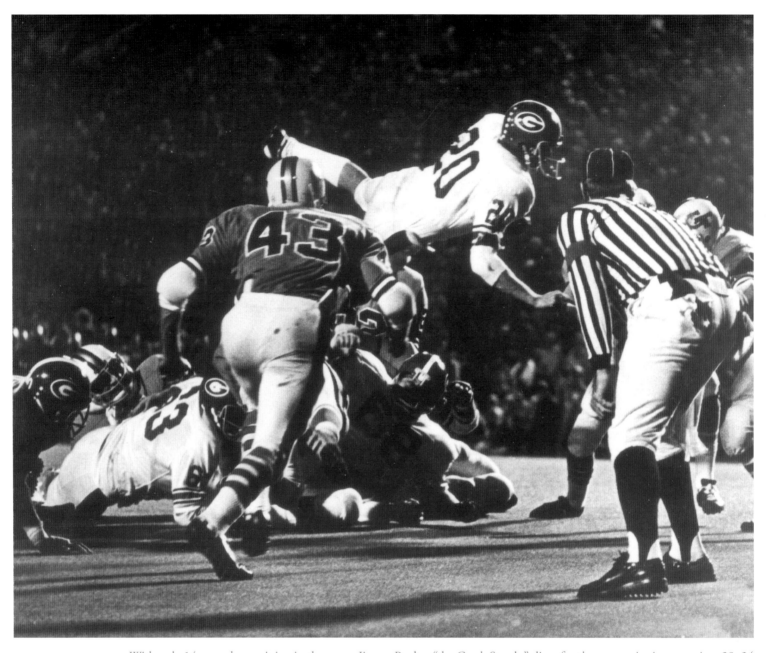

With only 14 seconds remaining in the game, Jimmy Poulos, "the Greek Streak," dives for the game-winning score in a 28–24 victory over Georgia Tech in 1971. The touchdown capped an 11-play, 65-yard drive that came in the game's final minute and a half. Poulos followed his 152-yard rushing effort against the Yellow Jackets with 161 yards against North Carolina in the Gator Bowl.

Royce Smith was the starting offensive right guard from 1969 to 1971. He was honored as a first team All-SEC selection as both a junior and senior and consensus All-American in 1971—Georgia's only consensus All-American in a six-season span from 1969 to 1974. The eighth overall selection by the New Orleans Saints during the 1972 NFL Draft, Smith remains the only Bulldog offensive lineman ever selected in the top 10 of the draft.

Aided by tailback Jimmy Poulos, quarterback James Ray looks for running room. Primarily a backup for three years, Ray was considered by Coach Vince Dooley to be "the best number two quarterback in the nation." From 1970 to 1972, the Columbia, South Carolina, native passed for 1,461 yards and 7 touchdowns. Ray also rushed for 418 yards, including 151 yards in a 24–0 victory over South Carolina in 1971.

Mixon Robinson was a reserve offensive and defensive end his first two seasons on the varsity team. As a senior in 1971, the Macon, Georgia, native played exclusively on defense and was selected as an All-SEC performer. Prior to the regular-season finale against Georgia Tech, Robinson was named the team's defensive captain. He would eventually become an orthopedic surgeon.

A starting tackle along Georgia's offensive line from 1969 to 1971, Tom Nash was a first team All-SEC selection as a junior and senior. In 1971, the same season he was an honorable mention Associated Press All-American, Nash was honored as just the sixth Bulldog ever to be chosen an Academic All-American.

Standing only 5-foot-7, Kim Braswell may have been small in stature, but he had a big, powerful kicking leg. Georgia's placekicker from 1970 to 1972, Braswell kicked a then Georgia-record 27 career field goals. His best-known kick was a 37-yard game winner against Florida in 1972, breaking a 7–7 tie with less than a minute remaining in the game.

Don Golden arrived at UGA from Valdosta, Georgia, as a quarterback; however, he was soon converted into a dual threat, defending the pass and punting the football. Golden was the Bulldogs' starting safety from 1971 to 1973 and primary punter as a junior and senior. His career average was nearly 40 yards per punt, and he intercepted 7 passes, including one returned 71 yards for a touchdown against Clemson in 1971.

In 1973, Bob Burns was described by Coach Vince Dooley as "the most versatile athlete we've had at Georgia in my 10 years here." A starting cornerback on the Bullpups' freshman team, Burns was moved to offense as a reserve flanker on the 1971 varsity squad. During his junior and senior seasons, Burns started at tight end, wingback, and fullback, ending his three-year career with nearly 1,000 yards rushing and receiving.

Freshman linebacker Sylvester Boler closes in on an Auburn back in 1973. "The Black Blur" recorded 18 tackles in the 28–14 win over the Tigers and was the main reason why Georgia's defense allowed just 142 total yards. After sitting out the majority of the season, Boler was making his first career start as a Bulldog. Two games later against Maryland in the Peach Bowl, he was named the bowl's most outstanding defensive player.

Nicknamed "Sky" by teammates because of his 6-foot-8 height, Craig Hertwig started at right tackle for the Bulldogs in 1973 and 1974. In his senior season, Hertwig earned All-SEC honors as well as being named first team All-American by the Associated Press.

After six years as Vanderbilt's head coach from 1967 to 1972 and an assistant with the New England Patriots for one season, Bill Pace was named Georgia's offensive coordinator in 1974. He instantly installed the veer offense, which the Bulldogs ran for four seasons until 1978.

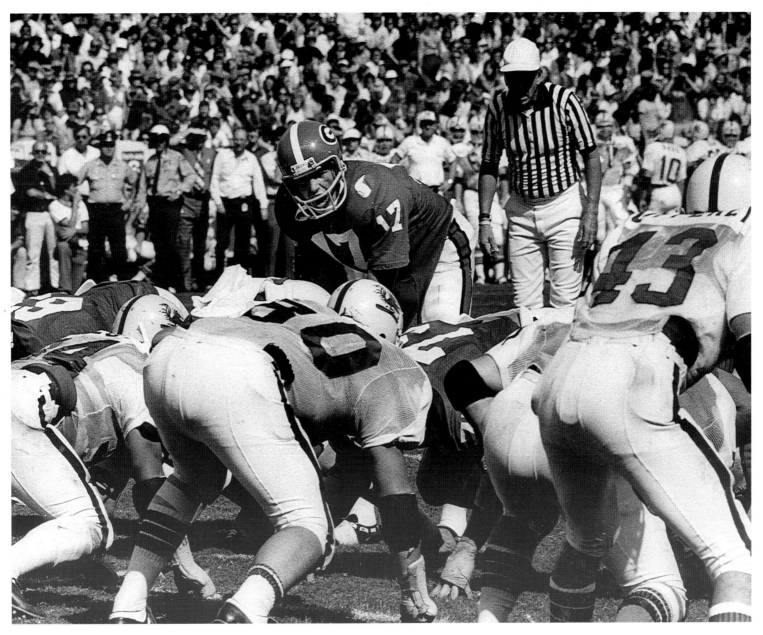

Against South Carolina in 1974, newcomer Matt Robinson quarterbacks Georgia's newly installed veer offense. The 502 rushing yards gained against the Gamecocks in a 52–14 win is still a single-game school record. Robinson, who gained 64 yards on 11 carries, was one of five Bulldogs to rush for more than 50 yards.

Seven of Georgia's nine first team All-Americans from 1970 to 1977 were offensive linemen, including guard Randy Johnson, a consensus selection in 1975. That same season, Johnson was a member of the "Canine Corps," a group of 10 team leaders established by head coach Vince Dooley.

Rusty Russell, son of renowned defensive coordinator Erk Russell, played under his father from 1973 to 1975. A starter at defensive end as a junior, Russell was moved to linebacker for his final year and ranked third in tackles with 90 on the "Junkyard Dogs" defensive unit. A Bulldog assistant in 1979 and 1980, Russell would eventually also coach at Memphis State, Central Florida, and Georgia Southern.

Linebacker Jim Griffith (no. 47) pressures Mississippi State quarterback Bruce Threadgill in a 28–6 Georgia victory in 1975. The sophomore and former walk-on recorded nine tackles in the game and spearheaded a defense that held a heralded rushing attack to 166 yards.

Despite his small stature and people frequently urging him to "give up," Hilton Young walked on at Georgia and eventually earned a scholarship. Only because the Bulldogs sustained injuries at the running back position, Young traveled with the team to Nashville to play Vanderbilt in 1975; it was his first time on an airplane. In only his second varsity game, Young rushed for two touchdowns in a 47–3 victory over the Commodores.

Quarterback Ray Goff (no. 10) chats with offensive coordinator Bill Pace on the sidelines during the mid-1970s. Goff's 1,434 rushing yards from 1974 to 1976 is an all-time second-best among Georgia quarterbacks. He is also one of only two Bulldog signal callers to finish in the Heisman Trophy's top ten in voting. In each of the six seasons Pace was UGA's offensive coordinator (1974-79), his offense averaged more than 195 yards rushing per game.

Early in the 1975 season, punter Bucky Dilts commented that Jacksonville's Gator Bowl was the toughest place to make a kick, because of its swirling wind. "You have to keep the ball lower than usual," said Dilts. Less than two months later, Dilts' 52-yard punt against Florida in Jacksonville was a pivotal play in Georgia's 10–7 victory. Aided by the fickle wind, the punt bounced sideways and out of bounds at the Gators' two-yard line. Dilts concluded his collegiate career in the 1977 Sugar Bowl at New Orleans' Superdome. In the Bulldogs' 27–3 loss to Pittsburgh, Dilts was one of the team's few bright spots, punting eight times for a 47.3 average. A year later, Dilts was a Denver Bronco and ended his rookie season punting in the very same dome against the Dallas Cowboys in Super Bowl XII.

When starting left guard and future All-American Joel Parrish was injured midway through the 1975 season, Hugh Hendrix (seen here) filled in admirably as the Bulldogs won six consecutive games to end the regular season. Less than two months before the start of the 1976 campaign, Hendrix died of a rare blood infection. The season was dedicated in his honor and the team responded by winning the SEC title.

Running back Al Pollard runs for a nice gain against California during the 1976 season opener. Georgia's 36–24 victory over the 15th-ranked Bears marked the first visit to UGA by a football team from California. Pollard finished the year third on the team in rushing, gaining 680 yards, including 100-yard performances in Georgia's final two regular-season games against Auburn (158) and Georgia Tech (112).

Trailing 27–13 at halftime against Florida in 1976, Ray Goff engineered Georgia's come-from-behind 41–27 win. The senior quarterback rushed for 124 yards and was responsible for 5 of the Bulldogs' 6 touchdowns. Since Goff's outing against the Gators, only twice has a Georgia quarterback rushed for 100 yards or more in a single game.

For the first two games of the 1974 season, sophomore Dicky Clark was the team's starting quarterback; however, by the end of the year, he had been demoted to third string. Prior to his junior season, Clark was moved to defensive end, where he excelled in his final two seasons. He recorded a combined 121 tackles in 1975 and 1976 and was named first team All-SEC as a senior.

It was said Joel "Cowboy" Parrish came to UGA in 1973 in a pickup truck, a mouth full of Redman, and wearing a 10-gallon hat and cowboy boots. Three years later, the right guard was selected a preseason All-American despite playing in only six games the season before. Parrish lived up to the billing, receiving consensus All-American status in 1976.

Mike "Moonpie" Wilson evidently got his nickname from the shape of his face (he couldn't stand to eat moonpies). A starting offensive tackle in 1975 and 1976, he was a first team All-American his senior season. After one season in the Canadian Football League, Moonpie played for Cincinnati and Seattle of the NFL from 1978 through 1989.

Allan Leavitt was the first player Georgia ever offered a kicking scholarship. During his career, he made what was then an SEC record: six field goals, three kicked as a freshman in 1973, of 50 yards or more. Leavitt's favorite field goal was a 33-yarder with five seconds remaining to defeat Georgia Tech in 1976. Following the 13–10 victory over the Yellow Jackets, fans carried the kicker around the field for half an hour.

A 28-year-old Prince Charles is honored at halftime during the 1977 Georgia-Kentucky game. Coach Vince Dooley gives the prince a signed football, reading "To HRH (His Royal Highness) Prince Charles, from Georgia, 1976 SEC Champions." With the Bulldogs trailing 10–0 before an eventual 33–0 loss, Charles asked Dooley, "Since you're behind, I guess I better pull for you?"

After leading Georgia's junior varsity to a 20–12 victory over Georgia Tech in 1977, freshman Davy Sawyer was forced into the varsity game against the Yellow Jackets only two days later. The sixth-string quarterback at the start of the season and unfamiliar with all of the varsity team's pass routes, Sawyer was unexpectedly thrust into action because of four quarterbacks who had sustained injuries and one who was academically ineligible.

George Collins was moved to tight end as a sophomore in 1975 after playing offensive guard on Georgia's freshman team and in high school. In 1976, he moved back to guard where he started his final two seasons. Recognized as a first team All-American in 1977 by the *Sporting News,* Collins was considered by Bulldog coaches to be the team's most consistent offensive player as a senior.

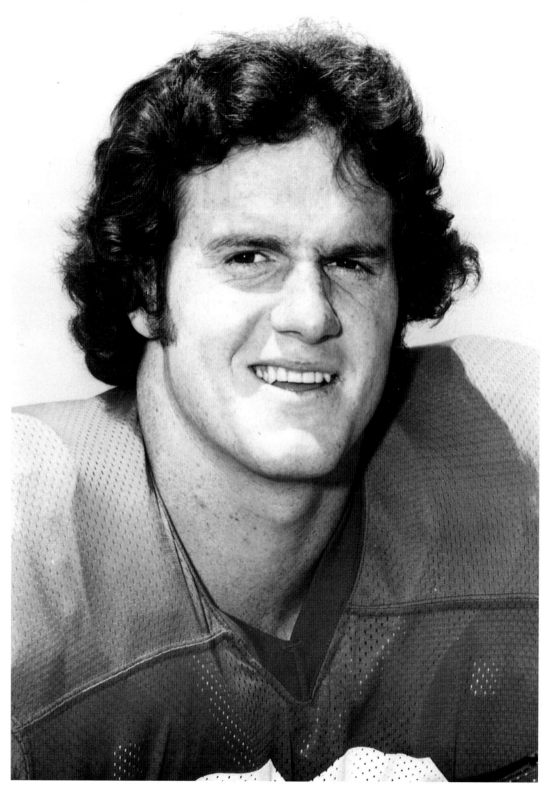

While earning All-SEC recognition during each of the three seasons (1975-77) he played on Georgia's varsity squad, roverback Bill Krug was a standout on the "Junkyard Dogs" defensive unit. Krug recorded 233 tackles as a Bulldog; his 13 sacks are still a school career record for a defensive back.

The Bulldogs were the only SEC school to recruit Ben Zambiasi, a diminutive fullback prospect out of Mount de Sales High School in Macon, Georgia. Zambiasi became a hard-hitting linebacker, leading the team in tackles and being named All-SEC his sophomore, junior, and senior seasons (1975-77). He is credited with a school-record 467 tackles during his career at Georgia.

In his lone year as Georgia's main running back, senior Willie McClendon started the 1978 season with eight consecutive 100-yard rushing games—the third-longest such streak in school history. During an impressive 9-1-1 regular season for the Bulldogs, McClendon rushed for 1,312 yards.

Center Ray Donaldson (no. 53) and left guard Nat Hudson (no. 65) block during Georgia's 17–16 comeback win over Kentucky in 1978. Donaldson would be selected first team All-SEC the following year and would play 17 seasons in the NFL with the Colts, Seahawks, and Cowboys. As seen here, Georgia introduced red pants during the 1978 season, donning them in most of its away and neutral-sited games.

Junior Buck Belue finds running room against Vanderbilt in 1980 during a decisive victory for the Bulldogs. Against the Commodores, Belue completed 7 of 11 passes for 139 yards, 1 touchdown, and won his 11th game as a starting quarterback for Georgia. The Valdosta, Georgia, native finished his collegiate career the following season with a remarkable 27-4 record as a starter and remains the only Bulldog to quarterback the school to back-to-back conference championships.

Trailing 21–20 to Florida in 1980 with only a minute twenty remaining in the game, the Bulldogs had the ball on their own seven-yard line, facing third down and 11 to go. Quarterback Buck Belue threw a short pass to Lindsay Scott (no. 24 in white), who turned it up field and ran for a 93-yard score and immortality. It is considered the greatest play in the history of Georgia football.

Mike Castronis, cheerleading coach from 1972 to 1986, was much more than an All-American lineman and longtime assistant. He has been called one of the greatest Georgia Bulldogs of all time, and perhaps their top ambassador.

The legendary voice of Larry
Munson is just as much part of
the celebrated history of Georgia
football as its greatest players,
coaches, and traditions. Munson
was the team's play-by-play radio
man from 1966 until early in the
2008 season. Perhaps his most
acclaimed and recognizable call is
the Buck Belue–to–Lindsay Scott
pass play that defeated Florida in
1980, when Munson begged the
receiver to "Run, Lindsay, Run!"

Freshman phenomenon Herschel Walker had an instant and tremendous impact on the 1980 Bulldogs. Walker's 1,616 rushing yards was an NCAA record for freshmen, his 283 yards against Vanderbilt remains a school single-game record, and, in rushing for 150 yards and 2 touchdowns in the Sugar Bowl, he was instrumental in Georgia's victory over Notre Dame for the national championship.

Seen here during the early 1980s, Coach Vince Dooley revamped the Bulldogs from one of the SEC's worst teams to one of its best. In the 15 seasons prior to Dooley's arrival, Georgia had only five winning campaigns. In his first five years in Athens, Dooley's Dogs won two SEC titles. The coach's best run was from 1980 to 1983, when the Bulldogs compiled a 43-4-1 record, captured three conference titles, and won the 1980 national championship.

NOTES ON THE PHOTOGRAPHS

These notes, listed by page number, attempt to include all aspects known of the photographs. Each of the photographs is identified by the page number, photograph's title or description, photographer and collection, archive, and call or box number when applicable. Although every attempt was made to collect all data, in some cases complete data may have been unavailable due to the age and condition of some of the photographs and records.

II RONNIE JENKINS IN ACTION
University of Georgia
jenkins

VI COACH DOOLEY VICTORY RIDE
University of Georgia
dooley.dodd

X GEORGIA'S "DREAM BACKFIELD," 1942
University of Georgia
mcphee (third from left)

2 FIRST GEORGIA TEAM
University of Georgia
1892team

3 THE 1893 SQUAD
University of Georgia
1893team

4 FIRST TEAM TO DEFEAT AUBURN
University of Georgia
1894team

5 COACH GLENN "POP" WARNER
University of Georgia
warner

6 RICHARD VONALBADE GAMMON
University of Georgia
gammon

7 THE CHAPEL BELL TRADITION
University of Georgia
chapel.bell

8 MARVIN DICKINSON
University of Georgia
dickinson

9 CHARLES BARNARD'S 1904 SQUAD
University of Georgia
1904team

10 HAROLD "WAR EAGLE" KETRON
University of Georgia
ketron

11 FIRST ALL-AMERICAN BOB MCWHORTER
University of Georgia
McWhorter.Bob.566

12 COACH ALEX CUNNINGHAM
University of Georgia
alex_cunnignham

13 QUARTERBACK DAVID PADDOCK
University of Georgia
paddock

14 ARTIE PEW
University of Georgia
pew

15 THE UNDEFEATED 1920 SQUAD
University of Georgia
1920team

16 COACH HERMAN STEGEMAN
University of Georgia
stegeman1

17 GEORGIA-OGLETHORPE GAME PROGRAM COVER
University of Georgia
day

18 STEGEMAN'S 1921 BULLDOGS
University of Georgia
1921team

19 TACKLE JOE BENNETT
University of Georgia
bennett

20 GEORGE "KID" WOODRUFF
University of Georgia
woodruff

21 IVY "CHICK" SHIVER
University of Georgia
Shiver_Ivy M. (Chick)

22 FIRST CONSENSUS ALL-AMERICAN TOM NASH
University of Georgia
Nash_Tom

23 GLENN LAUTZENHISER
University of Georgia
lautzenheiser

24 JOE BOLAND
University of Georgia
boland

25 RALPH "RED" MADDOX
University of Georgia
Maddox

26 SANFORD FIELD
PRACTICE SESSION
University of Georgia
herty field

28 AERIAL VIEW OF
SANFORD STADIUM,
1929
University of Georgia
sanford stadium 1929

29 END VERNON
"CATFISH" SMITH
University of Georgia
Smith Catfish

30 THE SANFORD
STADIUM HEDGES
University of Georgia
hedges

32 FRANK JOHNSON
University of Georgia
johnson_frank

33 PETE TINSLEY
University of Georgia
tinsley.pete

34 LEGEND FORREST
"SPEC" TOWNS
University of Georgia
towns

35 ALL-AMERICAN BILL
HARTMAN
University of Georgia
hartman

36 COACH HARRY MEHRE
University of Georgia
mehre

37 QUINTON LUMPKIN
University of Georgia
lumpkin

38 COACH JOEL HUNT
University of Georgia
hunt

40 VASSA CATE IN
ACTION
University of Georgia
cate

41 TEAM CAPTAIN
HEYWARD ALLEN
University of Georgia
allen

42 FRANK SINKWICH
University of Georgia
Sinkwich vs TCU 42 Orange

43 LAMAR "RACEHORSE"
DAVIS
University of Georgia
davis.lamar

44 CHARLEY TRIPPI AND
FRANK SINKWICH
University of Georgia
trippi and sinkwich

45 THE HEISMAN
WINNER, 1942
University of Georgia
sinkwich

46 GEORGE POSCHNER
University of Georgia
Poschner_George

47 VAN DAVIS
University of Georgia
davis_van

48 THE BULLDOGS ROSE
BOWL BOUND, 1942
University of Georgia
1942 bulldogs

50 COACH ALEX
CUNNINGHAM
University of Georgia
alex_cunningham

51 HARRY "KOON"
KUNIANSKY
University of Georgia
kuniansky

52 ALL-SEC WALTER
"CHIEF" RUARK
University of Georgia
ruark

53 HERB ST. JOHN
University of Georgia
st.john

54 CAPTAIN MIKE
CASTRONIS
University of Georgia
Castronis_Mike (2)

55 THE BULLDOGS
VERSUS ALABAMA,
1946
University of Georgia
rose_trippi

56 THE POTENT 1946
BACKFIELD
University of Georgia
Donaldson John(farleft31)

57 GEORGE JERNIGAN
University of Georgia
jernigan

58 STARTERS FOR THE
1946 SQUAD
University of Georgia
1946 bulldogs

59 DAN EDWARDS IN
ACTION
University of Georgia
edwards_dan 13404

60 THE 1948 BULLDOGS
University of Georgia
1948team

61 BERNIE REID
University of Georgia
reid

62 WEYMAN SELLERS
University of Georgia
sellers_w

63 "JARRING" JOHNNY
RAUCH
University of Georgia
Rauch1

64 JOE GERI
University of Georgia
geri

65 ELI MARICICH
University of Georgia
maricich

66 PORTER PAYNE
University of Georgia
payne

67 KEN MCCALL
University of Georgia
mccall

68 COACH DAN MAGILL
University of Georgia
dan magill

**69 BILLY MIXON, THE
"TIFTON TORNADO"**
University of Georgia
mixon

**70 COACH WALLY BUTTS
AND STAFF, 1950
SEASON**
University of Georgia
sterling dupree and shug j

71 ART DECARLO
University of Georgia
decarlo

72 BOBBY WALSTON
University of Georgia
walston

73 ZIPPY MOROCCO
University of Georgia
morocco

**74 ALL-SEC FRANCIS
MARION CAMPBELL**
University of Georgia
campbell

75 LAUREN HARGROVE
University of Georgia
hargrove

**76 BRONZE OF MIKE THE
MASCOT**
University of Georgia
mike statue

77 HARRY BABCOCK
University of Georgia
Babcock Harry

**78 JIMMY CAMPAGNA,
THE "ROCHESTER
ROCKET"**
University of Georgia
campagna

79 ZEKE BRATKOWSKI
University of Georgia
Bratkowski.Zeke.0023

80 JOHN CARSON
University of Georgia
Carson Johnny

81 COACH WALLY BUTTS
University of Georgia
butts

**82 BOB "FOOTS"
CLEMENS**
University of Georgia
clemens

83 BOBBY GARRARD
University of Georgia
garrard

84 KNOX CULPEPPER
University of Georgia
culpepper

85 UGA THE FIRST
University of Georgia
Uga.1.34

86 KEN COOPER
University of Georgia
Cooper Ken

87 JIMMY ORR
University of Georgia
orr

88 J. B. DAVIS
University of Georgia
davis_jb

**89 CHARLEY BRITT AND
THERON SAPP IN
ACTION**
University of Georgia
Sapp2

90 NAT AND PAT DYE
University of Georgia
Dye, Pat and Natt

**91 RIGHT TACKLE NAT
DYE**
University of Georgia
Dye Natt2

92 CHARLEY BRITT
University of Georgia
Britt Charley

93 DON SOBERDASH
University of Georgia
soderbash

94 DON LEEBERN
University of Georgia
leebern

**95 BILL "TATER-BUG"
GODFREY**
University of Georgia
godfrey_bill

96 JIMMY VICKERS
University of Georgia
vickers

97 BILL HERRON
University of Georgia
herron

98 "FLYIN' FRED" BROWN
University of Georgia
brown.fred

99 FRAN TARKENTON
University of Georgia
Tarkenton.Fran.101

100 PAT AND NAT DYE
University of Georgia
Dye, Pat and Natt2

**101 DURWARD
PENNINGTON AND
BOBBY WALDEN**
University of Georgia
walden

**102 BOBBY GREEN IN
ACTION**
University of Georgia
mckenny

103 GUARD PAT DYE
University of Georgia
dye

104 THE BUTTS LEGACY
University of Georgia
ears whitworth2

106 PETE CASE
University of Georgia
case

107 LARRY RAKESTRAW
University of Georgia
rakestraw

108 COACH JOHNNY
GRIFFITH
University of Georgia
griffith

109 "BIG JIM" WILSON
University of Georgia
Wilson_Jim

110 BOB ETTER
University of Georgia
etter

111 RAY RISSMILLER
University of Georgia
Rissmiller1

113 PRESTON RIDLEHUBER
IN ACTION
University of Georgia
ridlehuber

114 LYNN HUGHES
University of Georgia
hughes

115 "BULLET" BOB TAYLOR
University of Georgia
taylor.bob

116 PAT HODGSON
University of Georgia
hodgson

117 PASSING THE COLLAR
TO UGA II
University of Georgia
Uga.II.38

118 RONNIE JENKINS IN
ACTION
University of Georgia
jenkins

119 GEORGE PATTON
University of Georgia
Patton_George

120 DENNIS HUGHES
University of Georgia
hughes1

121 EDGAR CHANDLER
University of Georgia
Chandler Edgar

122 TERRY SELLERS
University of Georgia
sellers_t

123 STERLING DUPREE
WITH PLAYERS
University of Georgia
sterling_dupree2

124 DEFENSIVE
COORDINATOR ERK
RUSSELL
University of Georgia
erk russell

126 KIRBY MOORE
University of Georgia
moore.kirby

127 THE 1968 BULLDOGS
WITH COACH DOOLEY
University of Georgia
1968 bulldogs

128 BILLY PAYNE
University of Georgia
payne.billy

129 ROBERT "HAPPY"
DICKS
University of Georgia
dicks

130 JIM MCCULLOUGH
University of Georgia
mccullough

131 BILL STANFILL
University of Georgia
Stanfill1

132 JAKE SCOTT
University of Georgia
scott.jake.0002

133 GEORGIA
CHEERLEADERS,
1960S
University of Georgia
cheer1

135 MIKE CAVAN IN
ACTION
University of Georgia
Cavan Mike3

136 STEVE GREER
University of Georgia
Greer1

137 CHEERLEADERS IN THE
VANGUARD
University of Georgia
cheer2

138 PETER RAJECKI AND
SAM MRVOS
University of Georgia
rajecki

139 CHARLIE WHITTEMORE
University of Georgia
whittemore

140 TOMMY LYONS
University of Georgia
Lyons_Tommy

142 CHUCK KINNEBREW
University of Georgia
kinnebrew

143 CLARENCE POPE
University of Georgia
pope

144 LARRY WEST
University of Georgia
west

145 HORACE KING
University of Georgia
king

146 ROOTING FOR THE
TEAM
University of Georgia
cheer3

147 BUZY ROSENBERG IN
ACTION
University of Georgia
rosenberg.buzy

148 JIMMY SHIRER
University of Georgia
shirer

149 ERK RUSSELL WITH
JERONE JACKSON
University of Georgia
erk russell5

150 JIMMY POULOS, "THE
GREEK STREAK"
University of Georgia
poulous

151 ROYCE SMITH
University of Georgia
Smith Royce

152 JIMMY POULOS AND JAMES RAY IN ACTION
University of Georgia
ray

153 MIXON ROBINSON
University of Georgia
robinson

154 TOM NASH
University of Georgia
nash.tom

155 KIM BRASWELL
University of Georgia
braswell.kim

156 DON GOLDEN
University of Georgia
golden

157 BOB BURNS
University of Georgia
burns

158 SYLVESTER BOLER, "THE BLACK BLUR"
University of Georgia
boler

159 CRAIG "SKY" HERTWIG
University of Georgia
Hertwig_Craig

160 OFFENSIVE COORDINATOR BILL PACE
University of Georgia
bill pace1

161 MATT ROBINSON IN ACTION
University of Georgia
robinson_matt

162 RANDY JOHNSON
University of Georgia
Johnson Randy2

163 RUSTY RUSSELL
University of Georgia
russell_rusty

164 JIMMY GRIFFITH
University of Georgia
griffith

165 HILTON YOUNG
University of Georgia
young

166 RAY GOFF WITH BILL PACE
University of Georgia
bill pace2

167 BUCKY DILTS
University of Georgia
dilts

168 HUGH HENDRIX
University of Georgia
hendrix

169 AL POLLARD IN ACTION
University of Georgia
pollard

171 RAY GOFF IN ACTION
University of Georgia
goff1

172 DICKY CLARK
University of Georgia
clark

173 JOEL "COWBOY" PARRISH
University of Georgia
parrish

174 MIKE "MOONPIE" WILSON
University of Georgia
Wilson_Mike

175 ALLAN LEAVITT
University of Georgia
Leavitt Allen

176 COACH DOOLEY WITH PRINCE CHARLES
University of Georgia
dooley.princecharles

177 DAVY SAWYER
University of Georgia
sawyer

178 GEORGE COLLINS
University of Georgia
Collins_George

179 BILL KRUG
University of Georgia
krug

180 BEN ZAMBIASI
University of Georgia
Zambiasi Ben

181 WILLIE MCCLENDON
University of Georgia
mcclendon.willie

182 RAY DONALDSON AND NAT HUDSON IN ACTION
University of Georgia
donaldson3

183 SCOTT WOERNER
University of Georgia
woernertech78

184 AMP ARNOLD IN ACTION
University of Georgia
arnold.amp

185 DAVID ARCHER
University of Georgia
archer

186 JOEL EAVES AND VINCE DOOLEY
University of Georgia
eaves and dooley

187 MATT BRASWELL
University of Georgia
braswell_matt

188 JEFF PYBURN IN ACTION
University of Georgia
pyburn

189 MATT SIMON IN ACTION
University of Georgia
simon

190 REX ROBINSON IN ACTION
University of Georgia
robinson.rex

191 BOB KELLY
University of Georgia
kelly.bob

192 STEVE KELLY
University of Georgia
kelly.steve

193 JIMMY PAYNE AND NATE TAYLOR
University of Georgia
payne.jimmy

194 Uga III
University of Georgia
Uga.III.65

195 Buck Belue in Action
University of Georgia
belue.buck

196 Lindsay Scott in Action
University of Georgia
scott

197 Mike Castronis as Cheerleading Coach
University of Georgia
mike_castronis2

198 Larry Munson, on the Radio
University of Georgia
munson 6101

199 Herschel Walker
University of Georgia
herschel_walker

200 The Vince Dooley Legacy
University of Georgia
dooley_vince1557